Notre Dame College of Education

(English Dpt.)

Bearsden

An Introduction to Systemic Linguistics
1 Structures and Systems

An Introduction to Systemic Linguistics

1 Structures and Systems

Margaret Berry

Lecturer in the Department of English,
University of Nottingham

B. T. BATSFORD LTD London

First published 1975

Second impression 1977

© Margaret Berry 1975

Made and printed in Great Britain by
Billing & Sons Ltd., Guildford, London and Worcester

for the publishers B. T. Batsford Ltd, 4 Fitzhardinge Street, London W1H OAH

ISBN 0 7134 2902 x (hardcover edition)
ISBN 0 7134 2903 8 (paperback edition)

To H.R.B. and C.E.B.

Contents

Preface

This book is intended for students in English departments of universities and colleges of education. It aims at introducing such students to one kind of linguistics, the kind which is usually known as 'systemic linguistics'. Brief remarks are made at intervals in the book about ways in which this kind of linguistics differs from other kinds.

The book deals in turn with each of the most fundamental concepts of systemic linguistics, giving an explanation of each concept and discussing passages of English in relation to the concept. It is hoped in this way to familiarize students with the basic ideas of systemic linguistics, so that they will be able to read with comparative ease the more advanced books and articles on the subject. Suggestions for further reading are given in the bibliography of each chapter.

The book is divided into two volumes: Volume I, Structures and Systems; and Volume II, Levels and Links. Volume I deals with the two most basic categories of grammar, structure and system, and with other related grammatical concepts. Volume II deals with the levels of language other than grammar and discusses the relationships which exist between the categories within grammar and the relationships which exist between grammar and the other levels. The most important chapters in the book for an understanding of systemic linguistics are Chapters 8 and 9 of Volume I and Chapters 2 and 6 of Volume II, since these chapters deal with the concepts which most distinguish systemic linguistics from other kinds of linguistics.

I make no claim to originality. The ideas expressed are almost all those of other people, notably Professor J. R. Firth, Professor M. A. K. Halliday and Professor J. McH. Sinclair. I apologize to the original authors of the ideas, if I have in any way misrepresented them in my attempt to make the ideas easily intelligible to people who have little or no prior knowledge of linguistics.

I should like to thank all those who, directly or indirectly, have helped in the writing of the book: Professor M. A. K. Halliday, Professor J. McH. Sinclair and Mr J. G. Williamson who read the first draft and made numerous extremely helpful comments and who have also given a great deal of general help and encouragement; others who read and commented on parts of the first draft, including Dr R. A. Hudson and Dr R. I. Page; students, friends and colleagues at the University of Nottingham 1960–73, discussions with whom have been invaluable, especially Mr D. Evans, Mr C. S. Butler, Mr B. J. Calder, Dr R. G. Keightley, Mr W. Nash, Dr R. R. K. Hartmann and Mr C. J. Pountain; Professor P. Hodgson and Mrs V. G. Salmon of Bedford College, University of London, who first encouraged my interest in linguistics; Professor K. Cameron and Professor J. Kinsley of the University of Nottingham who made it possible for me to follow up this interest; and my mother and father, who have helped by typing the manuscript, drawing diagrams and checking proofs, and whose general encouragement has been even more valuable than their active assistance in the preparation of the book.

In spite of all the assistance which I have received, there still remain many faults in the book. For these I am, of course, solely responsible.

1
Introducing Linguistics

1.1 WHAT IS LINGUISTICS?

Linguistics is the study of language.

Language can be studied from a number of different points of view. Linguistics can accordingly be subdivided into a number of different kinds of linguistics. For instance, *general linguistics, descriptive linguistics, contrastive linguistics* and *applied linguistics* each show a rather different kind of interest in language.

1.1.1 *General Linguistics*

General linguistics, or theoretical linguistics as it is sometimes called, is the study of the nature of language. Questions which are of central interest in general linguistics are: What is language? How does language work? What have all languages got in common?

1.1.2 *Descriptive Linguistics*

Whereas general linguistics is interested in language in general, in what all languages have in common, descriptive linguistics is interested in particular languages and their individual characteristics. A descriptive linguistic study might, for instance, be an account of the English Language or an account of the French Language. The aim of such a study would be to describe the particular language in the best possible way; that is, in the way that best represented the various patterns observable in the language.

Or a descriptive study might be concerned with a particular variety of a language rather than with a language as a whole. It might be an account of a particular *dialect* of a language. It might be an account of a regional dialect: the language of the North Riding of Yorkshire, for example, or the language of Devonshire; or it might be an account of a social dialect: the language of a particular social class; or it might be an account of an age dialect: the language used by a particular age group.

A descriptive study might be an account of a particular *register* of a language. Registers, like dialects, are varieties of a language. Dialects are varieties of a language which depend on the user of the language. Registers are varieties of a language which depend on the use of the language. We speak whatever dialect we speak because of who we are, where we were born, where we were brought up, where we were educated, where we have been since, how old we are. We speak whatever register we speak because of what we are doing at a given time. We use a different register when we are chatting to friends from the register that we use when making an after-dinner speech. We use a different register when writing a friendly letter from the register that we use when writing an essay. The register we use will depend on a number of factors: on whether we are speaking or writing, on what we are speaking or writing about, on who we are speaking or writing to, on why we are speaking or writing. Descriptive studies which have so far been made of registers of English include an account of the language of advertising (Leech, 1966), and an account of scientific English (Huddleston *et al.*, 1968). Some attempts have also been made to describe the language of literature (e.g. Leech, 1969).

A descriptive study might be an account of the language of a particular historical period. It might be a description of Old English, for instance, or a description of sixteenth-century English.

A descriptive study might be an account of a particular *idiolect*; that is, an account of the language used by one particular individual.

Or it might be an account of a particular *text*, an account of a particular stretch of language. It might, for instance, be a description of the language of a particular poem or a description of the language of a particular conversation. (The term *text* can be used to refer to a stretch of spoken language as well as to a stretch of written language.)

Though different, general linguistics and descriptive linguistics should not be thought of as completely separate activities. There are important links between them. Descriptive studies of particular languages and particular varieties of languages help to provide answers to the general linguistic questions: What is language? How does language work? What have all languages got in common? A linguist's views on what language is and how language works influence the way in which he describes particular languages and particular varieties of languages.

1.1.3 Contrastive Linguistics

Having described two or more particular languages, a linguist can then, if he so wishes, go on to compare them in such a way as to bring out the differences between them. Or he can compare the language of two or more historical periods in order to show the historical development of a language. Or he can compare two or more dialects, or two or more registers. He can compare two or more idiolects, or two or more texts.

1.1.4 Applied Linguistics

General linguistics, descriptive linguistics and contrastive linguistics are all interested in language or languages for their own sake, because language and languages are interesting subjects for study. For all these kinds of linguistics the answer to the question 'Why study language?' is rather like the answer to the question 'Why climb Everest?': because it's there; because it's an interesting and enjoyable thing to do. The study of language and languages is a rewarding and worthwhile study in its own right.

Applied linguistics has other motives for studying language in addition to an interest in language itself. As well as being concerned with questions relating to language—What is language? How does language work? What have all languages got in common? What are particular languages and varieties of languages like? How do they differ?—applied linguistics is also interested in other questions, questions which are usually the concern of some discipline other than linguistics.

There are a number of fields of study in which language questions are at present being considered in relation to questions from other disciplines. Five of these fields will be considered here: *psycholinguistics, sociolinguistics, communication engineering, stylistics,* and *linguistics and language teaching.*

(It should be noted that the terms *contrastive linguistics* and *applied linguistics* are being used in this book in their widest possible senses. Each of the two terms is often used in a much narrower sense, *contrastive linguistics* to refer to a particular kind of comparison between two languages, *applied linguistics* to refer just to the field of linguistics and language teaching.)

1.1.4.1 *Psycholinguistics*

Psycholinguistics is the field of study which considers linguistic questions and psychological questions in relation to each other. One question which is both a linguistic question and a psychological question is: How do we acquire language?

1.1.4.2 *Sociolinguistics*

Sociolinguistics is the field of study which considers linguistic questions and sociological questions in relation to each other. One question which is both a linguistic question and a sociological question is: How far and in what ways does our social and cultural background condition the way in which we use language?

1.1.4.3 *Communication Engineering*

Certain engineering problems and certain linguistic problems are interdependent. For instance, attempts have been made to set up a system of machine translation. In order to make a machine translate from one language into another, one needs to know not only how machines work but also how language works. One also needs to know what the two languages in question are like and how they differ from each other.

1.1.4.4 *Stylistics*

Stylistics is the application of linguistics to the study of literature.

Literary scholars interested in the theory of literature or the theory of criticism are concerned with the questions: What is literary language? How does literary language work? These questions are, of course, closely related to the questions that concern general linguistics.

Literary scholars are also concerned to describe the language of literature, to see in what ways it is a register distinct from other registers and in what ways it overlaps with other registers.

Frequently literary scholars wish to describe the language used by a particular writer, an idiolect, or the language of a particular literary text. Often they wish to compare the language of two or more writers or the language of two or more literary texts.

Literary scholars vary in their assessment of the usefulness of linguistics to literary studies. Some have found that a linguistic consideration of a poem, or other literary text, has given them insights into the language of the text which have helped them to interpret and evaluate the text. Others prefer to rely on their own intuition for interpretation and evaluation, but have found that linguistic analysis provides them with evidence which they can offer in support of their intuitive judgements. Yet others have felt that the chief value of linguistics for them is that it helps them to put their intuitions into words. Linguistics has, in fact, sometimes been defined as 'a language for talking about language'. Some literary scholars have found that linguistics has helped them to express their observations about literary works more neatly, more precisely and less emotively than is often the case in critical writing. However, some literary scholars have found no use at all for linguistics.

1.1.4.5 *Linguistics and Language Teaching*
There are different kinds of language teaching. One basic distinction is between teaching people about language and teaching people to use language. Teaching people about language involves helping them to be consciously aware of the nature of language and of the patterns that are observable in particular languages and in particular varieties of languages. Teaching people to use language involves helping them to express themselves more effectively in speech and writing.

Teaching people to use language can be further subdivided into teaching people to use their own native language and teaching people to use a foreign language. Teaching people to use a foreign language includes the teaching of a country's language to the immigrant population of that country.

Teaching people about language really means teaching people linguistics, though of course, if one were dealing with young children, the linguistics that one would teach would be at a very elementary level. In order to help people to be aware of the patterns of particular languages one needs a vocabulary in which one can discuss such matters. Here again linguistics can provide a language for talking about language. (One would not, of course, want to introduce too much new terminology too quickly to young children.)

Not all teachers agree that it is necessary, useful or desirable to teach children about language. Most teachers do agree, however, that it is necessary to teach children to use their native language more effectively. Even if teachers do not believe in teaching linguistics, even elementary linguistics, to children, linguistics is still useful, indeed essential, for the teachers themselves.

A teacher who is teaching people to use their native language needs to know something about the nature of language, about the nature of the thing he is teaching. A teacher can do positive harm in language teaching if he is at the mercy of his own prejudices with no guidance from an understanding of the way in which a language works.

A teacher who is teaching people to use language also needs to be aware of the patterns of the particular language he is teaching. He must be aware, too, of the different varieties of that language and of the ways in which they differ. For instance, harm can be done at all levels of teaching if a teacher fails to realize the very great differences that exist between spoken language and written language. In particular, teachers teaching children to read must be aware of these differences. When children first attend school, a large number of them have no experience of written language, only of spoken language. Unless teachers are aware of the differences between the two they will have no idea of the problems confronting the children.

A teacher also needs to know something about language acquisition (psycholinguistics). It is no use trying to make someone learn a language in a way in which people never do learn language.

A teacher also needs to know something about the difference that social background can make to the use of language (sociolinguistics). Children from what are now frequently called 'disadvantaged' areas often use language in ways which differ from the ways in which their teachers use language, these differences being much more radical than just the use of different vocabulary items. Unless the teachers are aware of the differences, communication between themselves and the children will be impaired.

Like the teacher of a native language, the teacher of a foreign language needs to know something about the nature of language, something about the patterns of the particular language he is teaching, something about the different varieties of that language, something about language acquisition and something about language in relation to social background.

1.2   WHY IS LINGUISTICS SOMETIMES CALLED 'MODERN LINGUISTICS'?

At one time the term *linguistics* often used to occur with the adjective *modern* in front of it. It is perhaps worth considering what is modern about linguistics.

The term *linguistics* itself is modern in that it has only come into popular use during the twentieth century. The term refers to a twentieth-century brand of language study, language study which is in accordance with present-day views about language (1.2.1), with present-day views about how to study language (1.2.2) and, indeed, with present-day views about how to study anything (1.2.3).

It should not be assumed, however, that twentieth-century linguistics and earlier approaches to language study are mutually exclusive—far from it. A great number of the ingredients of modern linguistics go back to the ancient Greeks. What modern linguistics has done is to give new kinds of perspective to the old ingredients.

A number of criticisms of earlier approaches to language study will be made or implied in sections 1.2.1, 1.2.2 and 1.2.3. These criticisms for the most part apply, not to the best language scholars of earlier days, but rather to the rank and file. Unfortunately it has usually been the latter who have had the greatest influence on public opinion about language.

Modern linguistics should not be regarded as a reformation of language study. This would imply that it wanted to sweep away all the earlier approaches to language study, substituting supposedly better approaches in their place. It should be regarded rather as a rejuvenation of language study, bringing to the fore again all that was best in earlier language study and adding the new kinds of perspective mentioned above.

1.2.1 Present-day Views on Language

From the time of the ancient Greeks until quite recently, the majority (though not all) of the writers on language have been obsessed with questions of 'correctness': What are the 'correct' forms of language? Which forms are 'incorrect'? Is it 'correct' to split an infinitive? Is it 'correct' to say *It's me*? Most present-day writers on language no longer accept the concept of 'correctness' in relation to language. Of the various forms of language which are in general use, no one set of forms is considered to be any more 'correct' than any other set.

This does not mean that present-day writers on language are advocating linguistic anarchy, as they are sometimes accused of doing. They do accept the concepts of appropriateness and effectiveness. A particular form of language may not be any more 'correct' than another, but it may well be more appropriate than the other in a given situation. *Bung over the salt. Would you please pass me the salt?* Neither of these two utterances is any more 'correct' than the other. The first would be appropriate in a very informal situation. The second would be appropriate in a more formal situation. The first would be inappropriate in a formal situation. The second, if used in a very informal situation, would be likely to occasion the comment *'Ark at 'im!* Each is appropriate in its own situation. Each is inappropriate in the other's situation.

A particular form of language may also be more effective than another. If one form of language fails to communicate what it was intended to communicate, it is fair to suggest that another form of language might have been better.

The seekers after 'correctness' have often appealed to various 'authorities' in order to support their statements about what is 'correct' and what is 'incorrect'.

1.2.1.1 *Logic*

One of the 'authorities' to which they have appealed is logic. Language must be logical and regular, they have said, so we must remove from language any forms which are not logical and regular; we must not allow such things as double negatives, because they are illogical.

They were quite right to associate logicality and regularity with language, but they were wrong to assume that they had to make it logical and regular. Language already is logical and regular. But the rules which give it its logicality and regularity are so complex that the logicality and regularity are not always readily apparent. The logic which seekers after 'correctness' tried to apply to language was too simple and naive. Logic, like language, can manifest itself in different ways. The rules according to which some languages function do make double negatives become positives. The rules according to which other languages function make double negatives just strong negatives. Some dialects of present-day English function according to the former set of rules, some according to the latter. Old English and Middle English functioned according to the latter. Linguists of the present day have a much greater appreciation of the extent of the complexity of language than had earlier students of language.

1.2.1.2 *Reality*

From the time of the ancient Greeks there have been a large number of people who believed that language grew out of the universe and consequently mirrored reality. These people came to believe that language was fixed and immutable. To them, language, in the form in which they had learnt it, was God-given. Anyone who used language in a different way was committing heresy.

A few of the ancient Greeks, however, believed that language was an arbitrary set of symbols imposed on the universe by mankind. This is the view which is held by present-day linguists. Any word is a symbol of an aspect of reality. Which word symbolizes which aspect of reality is quite an arbitrary matter. Although there is logic in the internal relationships of a language (as discussed in 1.2.1.1), there is no logical relationship between a word and what it symbolizes. In English the word *dog* symbolizes the animal dog. There is no logical reason why it should do so. In French the word *chien* symbolizes the same animal. There is no affinity between the two words and yet they both symbolize the same animal equally successfully. Language is not a matter of instinct, but a matter of convention. We do not use a particular word because our instinct tells us that it must belong to a particular aspect of reality. We use it because we know that the conventions of a particular society have assigned the word to that aspect of reality. Present-day understanding of the arbitrariness and conventionality of language allows us to be more tolerant of linguistic usages other than our own. We no longer need to feel that someone is a heretic if they have speech habits different from ours; it is simply chance that makes them speak differently.

1.2.1.3 *Grammar Books*
Frequently seekers after 'correctness' have cited grammar books in support of their views on 'correct' and 'incorrect' forms of language. Too often the books they have cited have been books based on nothing more than their authors' prejudices about language. Because writers have felt that it would be nice if people used a particular form of language, they have said that it is 'correct' to use that form.

We no longer believe that something is necessarily 'correct' because it says so in a book. We now believe that a 'language is what people say, not what someone thinks they ought to say'.

1.2.1.4 *'What I Was Taught when I Went to School'*
Another 'authority' which is closely allied to the grammar book is 'what I was taught when I went to school'. The same objections are open to this kind of 'authority' as to the grammar book. Also, if 'when I went to school' was a long time ago, then 'what I was taught' is now likely to be out of date, even if it was sensible at the time. Language changes. Present-day writers on language accept that it changes, that it is inevitable that it should change. They see no point in trying to stop it changing. Of course language cannot change too much all at once or it will become unintelligible, but gradual change does no harm at all. Water is famous for finding its own level. Language, too, soon rights itself if any imbalance occurs. If a language loses any of its resources, it

soon acquires others in compensation. Just because young people of today speak differently from young people of fifty years ago, it does not mean that language has decayed or is decaying.

(Students of language of earlier periods did accept, in fact were extremely interested in, long-term changes, such as changes which took place between Old English and Middle English, but they did not accept, or were not interested in, the short-term changes which were going on all around them in their own day.)

1.2.1.5   *Latin*

For some reason or other, Latin has acquired a reputation for extreme logicality and regularity. Many writers on English and other modern languages have, out of patriotism, either pretended that their own languages were like Latin or, in the belief that their own languages were inferior to Latin, tried to make them more like Latin. It is to this brigade of seekers after 'correctness' that we owe the myths that it is wrong to split an infinitive and that it is wrong to say *It's me*.

It is ludicrous to apply the same criteria of evaluation to English as to Latin. The two languages belong to different kinds of language. Latin was basically a synthetic language; that is, it showed relationships between its words by adding inflexional endings to the words. English is basically an analytic language; that is, it shows the relationships between its words by placing other quite separate words, such as prepositions, near its main words. Latin shows that an infinitive is an infinitive by giving it a distinctive inflexional ending: *amare, orare*. English shows that an infinitive is an infinitive by placing *to* in front of it: *to love, to pray*. Latin forms other tenses of its infinitive by changing the ending: *amavisse, oravisse*. English forms other tenses of its infinitive by adding a separate auxiliary verb: *to have loved, to have prayed*. In Latin an infinitive consists of a single word, so of course it cannot be split. In English an infinitive usually consists of more than one word; it can be split.

1.2.1.6   *'Standard English'*

English seekers after 'correctness' have regarded the so-called 'Standard English'—the kind of English that gives no clue to the region to which the speaker belongs—as being the 'authoritative' kind of English. All the other dialects of English, both social and regional, have been regarded as deviations from 'Standard English' and, because they deviated from it, have been regarded as inferior to 'Standard English'.

All dialects of English are now regarded by linguists as being equally reputable. No dialect, not even 'Standard English', is any more 'correct' than any other dialect. However, there are occasions on which certain dialects are more appropriate or more effective than others. If one wishes to be understood by people from regions other than one's own, it is best to use a form of language which approximates to 'Standard English'. On the other hand, if one has been brought up to speak a regional dialect and if one is chatting with other people who speak the same regional dialect, it would be affectation to use a form of language which approximates too closely to 'Standard English'. A large number of people these days are bi-dialectal and can switch from 'Standard English' to regional dialect, or vice versa, according to the situation in which they find themselves.

Similarly, there are occasions on which certain social dialects are more appropriate or more effective than others. Again, if one is talking to people from the same social background as oneself, it would be affectation to use a social dialect other than one's own. But one sometimes does need to use a social dialect other than one's own. Some social dialects, for instance, are not as well adapted as others to the use of language in order to learn. This is why children from 'disadvantaged' areas often find it difficult to settle down at school; they are being required to use a social dialect other than their native dialect. Also, some social dialects are not as well adapted as others to the use of language in order to form certain kinds of social relationship. This again makes it difficult for some children when they first come to school.

1.2.1.7 *Written Language*

Written language has often been considered superior to spoken language. Because, when speaking, people do not follow the rules of written language, they have often been said to be using language in a 'lazy' or 'slovenly' manner. Attempts have been made to teach children to speak the same kind of language as they would write.

It is now recognized that spoken language and written language are equally regular, but that spoken language follows rules which differ from the rules of written language. The art of speaking well is very different from the art of writing well. Good written language would sound pompous and would often be difficult to understand if used in a spoken conversation. There are some situations in which spoken language more nearly approximates to written language than in others. The language of a political speech, for instance, would be more like written language than the language of a conversation (often, of course, a speech is written down before being delivered as spoken language), though even here it is usually true to say that a speech is likely to be more effective if the language it uses does not approximate too closely to written language.

1.2.1.8 *Literary Language*

Among written registers of language, literary language has often been put on a pedestal and other registers have been judged according to the extent to which they resembled literary registers.

Literary language is no longer accorded this pre-eminence. No one would deny, of course, that in certain situations, literary situations, literary language is supreme. But there are other situations in which literary language would be most inappropriate. The language of *Paradise Lost*, for instance, would be most unsuitable for a modern scientific report, just as the language of a modern scientific report would be most unsuitable for *Paradise Lost*.

Present-day linguists, then, believe all these 'authorities' to be false gods. They believe that the job of a linguist is to describe language exactly as it is, not to try to titivate language. They believe that all varieties of language are equally reputable and equally worthy of being described, though with the reservation that certain varieties are more appropriate and more effective in certain situations than in others.

Since present-day linguists believe that their job is to describe language exactly as it is, their approach to language is sometimes called the *descriptive approach*. The older approach is sometimes called the *prescriptive approach*, since earlier scholars were intent on prescribing the 'correct' forms of language.

1.2.2 *Present-Day Views on How to Study Language*

1.2.2.1 *Approaches to Language Study Should Be Varied*

Present-day linguists believe that there is, and should be, more than one way of studying language. Newcomers to linguistics sometimes consider it a weakness of the subject that there are different schools of linguistics, each considering language in a different way. It is, on the contrary, a strength of linguistics that there are these different approaches to the subject. Controversy is always a healthy sign. Language is so complex that no one approach can cover all its aspects. The different approaches are complementary rather than contradictory.

1.2.2.2 *Language Study Should Not Be Too Cut-and-Dried*

Just as it is possible to have different general approaches to language study, so it is possible within a single approach to arrive at different descriptions of a particular language or of a particular stretch of language. It used to be thought that grammar questions on 'O' level examination papers were the easiest to mark because answers to them were either right or wrong. It is no longer so easy to decide whether an answer is right or wrong, since it is now realized that language is so extremely complex that no one method of labelling will be equally satisfying for all stretches of language. Often one finds oneself faced with a situation in which two or three different labels could be considered applicable to one bit of language. This is a desirable, not an undesirable, state of affairs. One gains a greater insight into the bit of language by considering in turn the rival labels than one would if one could with confidence attach just one label and leave it at that. Which label, or combination of labels, one eventually decides to use is often not so important as what one has learnt about the language in the course of trying to come to a decision.

1.2.2.3 *Language Study Should Provide Insights*
Too often in the past, especially in schools, language study degenerated into a process of labelling just for the sake of labelling. Sentences were taken to pieces and subjects, verbs and objects were labelled as subjects, verbs and objects and that was the end of the study. No attempt was made to make use of the analysis in order to gain insight into the nature of language in general or into the distinguishing characteristics of a particular language, dialect, register or idiolect, and no attempt was made to relate the findings of the analysis to the findings of other disciplines such as psychology, sociology or literary criticism. Present-day linguists still do use a process of labelling, but the labelling is now seen as a means to an end, not as an end in itself.

1.2.2.4 *Language Study Should be Coherent*
In the past, language scholars have tended to concentrate on such things as etymology (the study of the origin of individual words) and diachronic phonology (the study of the ways in which individual sounds have changed through the ages). These studies are very interesting; but there is a lot more to language than they suggest. Language is a structured system. It does not just consist of a lot of little atomistic bits which are quite separate from and independent of each other. We not only need to know about individual sounds and individual words; we also need to know how all the individual sounds are related to each other to form a structured system of sounds and how all the individual words are related to each other to form a structured system of words.

We need to know how the structured system of sounds relates to the structured system of words. We need to know how these two aspects of language relate to other aspects of language. Recently there have been evolved theoretical frameworks for language study which do attempt to relate to each other the different aspects of language and to relate to each other all the individual bits of language which come under the heading of each aspect.

These theoretical frameworks give to language study a sense of perspective. It is unlikely that any one linguist at any one time will be working on more than one or two aspects of language. A linguist needs to know how his particular aspects of language fit into the general picture of language as a whole. From the point of view of applied linguistics, if one has an overall view of what one is studying, one has a much better idea of the relative importance of certain aspects of language study. One can then concentrate on the things that matter rather than wasting time over trivialities such as whether or not to split an infinitive.

1.2.2.5 *Language Study Should Be Consistent*

Earlier language scholars were accustomed, when classifying language, to make use of a very inconsistent and haphazard assortment of criteria. For instance, it was possible to find in one and the same book that a noun is a word which refers to a person or thing (classification by reference criteria), that a pronoun is a word which stands instead of a noun (classification by substitution criteria), and that a preposition is a word which stands in front of a noun (classification by positional criteria). Present-day linguists do still use a variety of criteria, but they like to make it clear which kind of criterion they are using on a given occasion and to be consistent in the use of that criterion. They distinguish between categories arrived at by different criteria. Having disentangled the various criteria, they can then relate them to each other again via one of the theoretical frameworks mentioned in 1.2.2.4.

1.2.2.6 *Language Study Should Be Explicit*

The fact that there are different approaches to language study (1.2.2.1) and that there is no one right description of a particular language or a particular stretch of language (1.2.2.2) does not mean that language study is vague and imprecise—far from it. Great stress is laid these days on the need to be explicit in language study. It is necessary to be explicit about which general approach one has selected and why one has selected it, about the description one has arrived at of a particular language or stretch of language and the criteria by which one has arrived at it, and about the precise meaning of the terms included in the description. Often, in order to be rigorously precise and explicit, linguists formalize their descriptions in terms of mathematical symbols and formulae.

1.2.2.7 Language Study Should Be Autonomous

In the past, the study of language has often been confused with other disciplines such as philology (the study of certain features of language in order to interpret literary texts of earlier periods), literary criticism, philosophy, psychology and anthropology. It is true that linguistics is related to these other disciplines in that to a certain extent it shares their subject matter and some of the questions relating to the subject matter. However, its aims and methods are quite different from these other disciplines. Now that it has been disentangled from these other disciplines it can be of greater use to them, since it can now offer to them a body of independent observations on matters which are of mutual interest. (It should perhaps be mentioned that not all linguists of the present day would agree that linguistics should be autonomous.)

1.2.3 Trends Which Are Common to Linguistics and the Studies of Other Disciplines

Linguistics is sometimes defined as 'the scientific study of language'. There is a good deal of justification for this definition, since linguistics does owe much of its methodology, and even some aspects of its theory, to the sciences.

However, linguistics is also something of a social science. Language is a social activity. It therefore lends itself to the kind of study which is carried on in the social sciences.

Traditionally, the study of language has been regarded as an arts subject. It still is, to some extent, an arts subject. It still relies very much on intuition, often the same kinds of intuition as are encouraged by the other arts subjects.

It is perhaps less easy now than it was at one time to distinguish between the arts, sciences and social sciences. They seem recently to have drawn closer together in their methods and in their attitudes towards their subjects. The sciences have become more like the arts in that scientists now recognize the extremely important part which intuition plays in their work. The arts have become more like the sciences in that arts scholars are now more willing to seek objective verification of their intuitions. The sciences have become more like the social sciences in that scientists are now more willing to talk in terms of probabilities rather than in terms of certainties. It is now possible to observe trends which are common to the development of many disciplines of different kinds. Linguistics shares a number of these trends.

1.2.3.1 *The Recognition of the Value of Synchronic Studies*

In nineteenth-century academic circles the historical or *diachronic* approach to language study was dominant. Scholars' main interest was in tracing the development of a language from one period to the next, and in tracing the development of a number of related languages from a parent language.

Other arts disciplines, such as literary study, philosophy and theology, have also until recently been primarily historical in their approach. This interest of the arts subjects in chronological development is perhaps related to the nineteenth-century scientific interest in evolution which stemmed from the writings of Darwin.

Most disciplines are still interested in chronological development and still regard a historical approach to their subject as a worthwhile approach. They no longer, however, regard the historical approach as the only worthwhile approach. Even history is no longer so chronological in its approach to its subject matter.

Linguistics, like other disciplines, is still interested in chronological development. The kind of linguistics known as *historical linguistics* is still a popular form of study. However historical linguistics is now considered to be only a small part of language study. There are many interesting aspects of language other than its development, and these are best approached through *synchronic* studies; that is, through studies of a language as it is at a given time without reference to its previous history. A synchronic study of present-day English, for instance, would be a study of the sounds and words and grammatical patterns which are found in the English of the present day, without reference to the sources of origin of the words and without reference to the ways in which the sounds and grammatical patterns have changed since Old English or Middle English. The previous history of present-day English, although interesting, is largely irrelevant if one is mainly concerned with the sociological or psychological aspects of present-day English, or if one is trying to persuade a machine to translate English into another language.

1.2.3.2 *The Growth of a Technical Vocabulary*

Most disciplines have developed a technical vocabulary of their own which is largely unintelligible to scholars from other disciplines. This applies not only to the sciences but also to arts disciplines. Linguistics has developed a technical vocabulary and so too have many of the other traditional arts subjects, although they do not always realize that they have done so. Literary critics are apt to look askance at linguists because of the 'jargon' that linguists use, without realizing that literary criticism too has a 'jargon': *mode, type, structure, texture, paranomasia, prolepsis* and *fugal* are just a few of the many technical terms used by literary critics.

It is necessary for a discipline to develop a technical vocabulary. For any serious academic study, precision of expression is essential. It must be possible to use a form of language in which each word refers to one concept and one concept only. Economy of expression is also an advantage. If a concept can be expressed by a single word rather than by a string of words, it will save time and also add cogency to a statement. In order to achieve precision and economy, scholars often need to invent new words or to redefine old words. (This development of a technical vocabulary is of course related to the desire to be explicit: 1.2.2.6.)

However, it is equally necessary for scholars to be able to translate from technical language into non-technical language when they are addressing scholars from other disciplines. They will inevitably lose in precision and economy by doing so, but will gain in intelligibility.

Technical registers of language, like all registers, are appropriate and effective in some situations but not in others.

1.2.3.3 *The Search for Objective Verification of Intuitions*
Linguists, like the scholars of other disciplines, do not regard their intuitive discoveries as truths or facts, but merely as hypotheses which need to be tested. In order to test their hypotheses, linguists have borrowed some procedures from the social scientists and some from the scientists. Like the social scientists, they conduct interviews and send out questionnaires in order to obtain information. Like the scientists, they carry out experiments and make observations. Also like the scientists, they use technical apparatus in order to record observations and in order to make measurements. Some linguists submit their hypotheses to the operations of symbolic logic in order to test them. Others submit their data to statistical techniques and sometimes make use of computers in order to process the statistical information.

1.2.3.4 *The Use of Models*
The term *model* has for the last few years been an extremely fashionable word in disciplines ranging from the sciences to education and theology.

What are models? The term can perhaps best be explained by means of examples. Examples from the sciences will be given first, since these will probably be more familiar to readers than examples from linguistics.

One kind of model used in the sciences is the hardware model. Hardware models are models made from actual concrete materials such as metals. For example, a scientist studying the action of waves on the seashore might build a tank, put water and sand into the tank, and arrange some mechanism to blow on the water. The contents of the tank would then be a model of the aspect of reality being studied by the scientist. The main features of the real-life situation—water, sand, wind —would be represented, and an attempt would be made to simulate the relationships which exist in real life between these features.

Another kind of model used in the sciences is the analogy. An analogy is an aspect of reality which is used as if it were a model of another aspect of reality. There are usually some features, and relationships between features, which are obviously similar in the two aspects of reality. The object of the exercise would be to discover if there were any further similarities. For instance, a scientist studying light waves or sound waves might use as an analogy the waves of the sea. He would be interested in discovering how far light waves or sound waves resembled the waves of the sea in their behaviour. He would certainly not assume automatically that light waves or sound waves behaved like sea waves. He would not say: sea waves behave in such and such a way; therefore light waves and sound waves must behave in the same way. He would take as his hypothesis that light waves or sound waves resembled sea waves, but the hypothesis would remain to be tested. He would be saying: sea waves behave in such and such a way; *do* light waves or sound waves behave in the same way? The analogy would have suggested to him a line of inquiry. It would not have provided him with an established fact.

A third kind of model used in the sciences is the theoretical model. A theoretical model is like a hardware model in that it attempts to represent the main features of an aspect of reality and also the relationships between these features. It is unlike a hardware model in that it is not made of concrete substances but is built of abstractions. A theoretical model can usually be thought of as a picture in words of the thing that is being studied. Readers are unlikely to be familiar with any scientific theoretical models. Perhaps the nearest thing to a theoretical model that their school general science courses will have acquainted them with will be something like Boyle's Law. Boyle's Law states that, provided the temperature is constant, the volume of a given mass of air will be inversely proportional to the pressure upon it. This is often represented as the equation *pressure* × *volume* = *constant* or $P \times V = K$. The equation is a theoretical model in that it represents in abstract terms the most important features of the situation being studied, and, by means of the symbols ×, = and *constant*, shows the relationship between these features. The function of a theoretical model is, like that of an analogy, to suggest a hypothesis, a line of inquiry. Once the hypothesis has been well tested without being disproved, it becomes a law, as in the case of Boyle's Law, a law being something which can be stated with reasonable certainty. But until it has been tested it remains a hypothesis.

(Needless to say, this account of the use of models in science is an oversimplification. Some scientists would want to distinguish many more kinds of model than those exemplified above. And some scientists use the term *model* in a narrower sense than that in which it is used here.)

Hardware models are not used as much in linguistics as in some other sciences. Perhaps the nearest thing we have to a hardware model is the speech synthesizer, a machine which can be made to produce sounds which approximate to human speech.

Analogies are of more general use in linguistics. Often linguistic theory has been developed and extended by the use of analogies. For instance, at one stage it was thought that the theory of grammar had reached a more satisfactory point than the theory of certain other aspects of language. Linguists then used grammar as an analogy for other aspects of language. They said, for instance: grammatical theory can be said to have certain main categories; does lexical theory (the study of the vocabulary of language) have the same main categories? If so, are the relationships between the categories the same as for grammar?

Also, in description, one language can be used as an analogy for another, or one variety of a language as an analogy for another. It is sometimes useful, for instance, to use present-day English as an analogy for Old English in order to suggest lines of inquiry into Old English. It must be remembered, however, that an analogy can only suggest lines of inquiry; it cannot provide established fact. This is where traditional grammarians went wrong when they tried to relate English, and other modern languages, to Latin. They were, in effect, using Latin as an analogy for English, but they failed to realize the essentially hypothetical nature of an analogy. They said: Latin behaves in such and such a way; English must behave in the same way and if it doesn't it ought to, so let's make it do so. What they should have said was: Latin behaves in such and such a way; *does* English behave in the same way?

Theoretical models are perhaps the most useful kind of model of all in linguistics. There are various kinds of theoretical model. We should perhaps distinguish here between outline theoretical models and detailed theoretical models.

The outline theoretical models each attempt to give a comprehensive and general view of what language is and how language works, showing all the main aspects of language and relating them to each other. These outline theoretical models are in fact the theoretical frameworks mentioned in 1.2.2.4. These outline theoretical models are useful for their breadth of vision and for the sense of perspective which they give, but they are not overall sufficiently detailed or sufficiently precise to be objectively verifiable. Certain aspects of each outline theoretical model have, however, been worked out in sufficient detail to be verifiable and these take the form of detailed models within the main model.

It is important to realize that models are ever changing, never fixed. Linguists are continually trying to represent language in a more revealing way and consequently are continually developing and modifying their models. At any given time a model is two-way looking: it is a record of the current thinking of a linguist (or school of linguists) about language (or an aspect of language), this thinking being based on the results of past investigations; it is also a basis for future investigations. When these future investigations have been carried out, the model itself will be modified to take account of any new insights into language which have resulted.

2
Introducing Systemic Linguistics

2.1 IN WHAT WAYS IS SYSTEMIC LINGUISTICS DIFFERENT FROM OTHER SCHOOLS OF LINGUISTICS?

As mentioned in 1.2.2.1, there are different schools of linguistics. This book is about one particular school, that of *systemic linguistics*. So far, the book has attempted to give a broad view of linguistics which could for the most part be said to apply to all schools of linguistics. It is now time to consider systemic linguistics in particular, and to ask what it has in common with other schools of linguistics and how it differs from other schools of linguistics.

Systemic linguistics is like other schools of linguistics in that it is concerned with general linguistic questions (1.1.1), in that it is interested in describing and comparing particular languages and varieties of languages (1.1.2 and 1.1.3), and in that it is interested in various applications of linguistics (1.1.4).

Systemic linguistics is like other schools of linguistics in that it adopts a descriptive approach to language as opposed to a prescriptive approach (1.2.1).

Systemic linguists, like other linguists, realize that there is more than one way of studying language (1.2.2.1). They themselves present one particular view of language but they accept that theirs is by no means the only possible view of language. Indeed, there are differences of opinion within the systemic school. All systemic linguists adopt the same general approach, but they differ in matters of detail. (For this reason the following paragraphs on the characteristics of systemic linguistics should be accepted as generalizations. Probably not all systemic linguists would agree with all the remarks that have been made.)

Systemic linguists accept that there is no one right description of a particular language or of a particular stretch of language (1.2.2.2).

Systemic linguistics is like other schools of linguistics in that it has as its ideals the ideals of insightfulness (1.2.2.3), coherence (1.2.2.4), consistency (1.2.2.5) and explicitness (1.2.2.6). Like other linguists, systemic linguists do not always succeed in living up to their ideals.

Systemic linguists agree that language study should be autonomous, though closely related to other disciplines (1.2.2.7).

Systemic linguistics, like other schools, appreciates the importance of synchronic studies (1.2.3.1), has developed a technical vocabulary (1.2.3.2) and attempts to seek objective verification of its hypotheses (1.2.3.3).

Like other schools, systemic linguistics has developed an outline theoretical model of language to serve as a record of its current thinking about language and to provide a coherent framework for its future investigations (1.2.3.4). It also makes use of other kinds of model.

It can be seen from these brief remarks that systemic linguistics has a very great deal in common with other schools of linguistics. In what ways does it differ?

The schools of linguistics with which systemic linguistics has most in common are perhaps those of stratificational grammar (e.g. Lamb, 1966) and tagmemics (e.g. Pike, 1967). The school of linguistics with which systemic linguistics has least in common is perhaps transformational-generative (TG) grammar (e.g. Chomsky, 1957), though it is probably fair to say that more marked resemblances can be seen between systemic linguistics and some of the more recent developments in transformational-generative grammar (e.g. Fillmore, 1968).

The following paragraphs attempt to indicate some of the main differences between systemic linguistics and transformational-generative linguistics.

2.1.1. *Systemic Linguistics Attaches Very Great Importance to the Sociological Aspects of Language*

Perhaps the most important distinguishing feature of systemic linguistics is the very high priority it gives to the sociological aspects of language.

Systemic linguistics has developed from scale-and-category linguistics, a kind of linguistics which was practised in the early years of the 1960s (e.g. Halliday, 1961). Scale-and-category linguistics owed a great deal to still earlier work, that of Professor J. R. Firth (e.g. Firth, 1957). It is to Professor Firth's interest in sociology that we can trace the present interest in the sociological aspects of language, although the interest of systemic linguists takes a rather different form from that of Professor Firth.

Questions which are of central interest to systemic linguists are: What are the social functions of language? How does language fulfil these social functions? Systemic linguists consider that the answers to these questions are vitally important ingredients of the answers to the questions: What is language? How does language work?

When describing languages or varieties of languages, systemic linguists use a model which they think will best enable them to discover how the forms of a language or variety of a language can be related to its social functions.

Systemic linguists are particularly interested in describing varieties of language which depend on social situation: registers and social dialects.

(It is perhaps fair to say that although in general the first chapter of this book gave a broad view of linguistics, it did show a systemic bias in one or two places. More attention was paid to the concept of register than would have been paid had the book been introducing some other schools of linguistics. More attention was paid to the concept of appropriateness of language to situation than would have been the case for some other schools.)

Because of its sociological emphasis, systemic linguistics is particularly appropriate for application to sociolinguistic studies. Via sociolinguistics it also has applications to language teaching. And since it is so much concerned with the functions of language it also has relevance for stylistics.

Systemic linguistics, then, gives a very high priority to the sociological aspects of language. It gives a relatively low priority to the psychological aspects of language. Transformational-generative grammar on the other hand gives a very high priority to the psychological aspects of language but a relatively low priority to the sociological aspects of language. (This does not mean that systemic linguists do not consider the psychological aspects of language important. It just means that they do not regard such aspects as their primary concern. However, recently one or two systemic linguists have begun to give a higher priority to the psychological aspects of language.)

2.1.2 Systemic Linguistics Views Language as a Form of 'Doing' Rather than as a Form of 'Knowing'

Ferdinand de Saussure, one of the greatest linguists of all time, distinguished between what he called *langue* and what he called *parole*

(Saussure, 1916). One of the explanations he gave of the difference between these is based on a musical analogy. He likened *langue* to a piece of music and *parole* to performances of that piece of music. Performances of a given piece of music can differ very markedly and yet underlying all of them is something constant, the piece of music itself. The *langue* of a language is the constant structure of the language underlying the *parole*, the actual utterances of that language made on particular occasions.

Systemic linguistics and TG linguistics are alike in recognizing the importance of Saussure's distinction. Both schools include in their linguistic theory concepts similar to *langue* and *parole*.

However each school has adapted Saussure's concepts and the two schools differ in their adaptations. They differ particularly in their views of *langue*, their views of *parole* being much more alike (though even here there are important differences).

Both schools see *parole* as the use a person actually makes of his language on particular occasions, as what the person actually 'does' linguistically. The two schools use different terms for this concept, TG linguists referring to it as *performance*, systemic linguists referring to it in terms of *actual linguistic behaviour*.

Where the two schools really differ most is in their view of *langue*, the constant which underlies the utterances that constitute *parole/* performance/actual behaviour: TG linguistics views the constant as a form of 'knowing', while systemic linguistics views it as a set of possibilities for 'doing'.

For TG linguists *langue*, which they call *competence*, is a person's knowledge of his language. The TG competence v. performance distinction, their version of the *langue* v. *parole* distinction, is really a 'knows' v. 'does' distinction.

For systemic linguists *langue*, which they call *linguistic behaviour potential*, is the range of options from which a person's language and the culture to which he belongs allow him to select, the range of possible things that he 'can do' linguistically. The systemic behaviour potential v. actual behaviour distinction, their version of the *langue* v. *parole* distinction, is really a 'can do' v. 'does' distinction.

The TG view of *langue* as 'knowing' is part of their interest in the psychological aspects of language. The systemic view of *langue* as possibilities for 'doing' and the attempt to define behaviour potential in relation to a context of culture are part of the systemic interest in the sociological aspects of language.

The TG concept of competence is probably farther from Saussure's *langue* than the systemic concept of linguistic behaviour potential. Competence is a property of the individual, while linguistic behaviour potential, like *langue*, is basically a property of a speech community.

2.1.3 *Systemic Linguistics Gives a Relatively High Priority to the Description of the Characteristics of Particular Languages and Particular Varieties of Languages*

Systemic linguistics, when compared with transformational-generative grammar, can be said to give a relatively high priority to the description of the characteristics of particular languages, particular varieties of languages, particular idiolects, particular texts; and a relatively low priority to the discovery of the characteristics that all languages have in common.

The word *relatively* is extremely important here, and indeed in the preceding and following subsections. Very often the differences between schools of linguistics can be seen as differences in degree rather than differences in kind. Both systemic linguists and transformational-generative linguists are interested both in investigating the characteristics of particular languages and in discovering the characteristics that all languages have in common. Both schools would, in fact, see the two activities as related activities, since the description of particular languages can lead to the discovery of characteristics universal to language and also since linguists' views of language in general influence their descriptions of particular languages. The difference between the two schools is very much a difference in emphasis, a difference in priority, rather than a difference in kind.

This is another reason why systemic linguistics is appropriate to stylistic studies. It is concerned with particular languages, particular varieties, particular idiolects, particular texts, for their own sake, not just because of what they can tell us about language in general.

2.1.4 *Systemic Linguistics Explains a Number of Aspects of Language in Terms of Clines*

It was explained in 1.2.2.2 that it is now realized that language is so extremely complex that it is difficult to be cut-and-dried when analysing language. One sets up categories for an analysis only to find that the categories are not as clear-cut as one might at first have thought. Some items of language fall quite clearly into one category or another, but other items seem to fall midway between two categories. The categories have fuzzy edges. They shade into each other.

Probably all linguists are alike in recognizing the fuzziness of their categories. But linguists vary in the importance they attach to this fuzziness when formulating their linguistic theory. Systemic linguists do attach quite a lot of importance to it and in order to refer to it, they find it useful to use the concept of a *cline*. A cline is a scale on which all the points shade into each other. One end is quite different from the other end but it is impossible to tell exactly where one end merges into the other. Systemic linguists often say of two categories that they are on a cline. When they say this they are recognizing that some items of language fall quite clearly into category A and that some items fall quite clearly into category B, but that some items fall at various points along the scale between A and B.

Clines are really continua. As has been said, all their points shade into each other. The recognition of continua may be highly desirable in theory, but for the purposes of practical description of languages, varieties of languages, etc., it is not possible to work with a continuum. It is not sufficiently explicit to say of an item of language that it falls somewhere on a continuum between category A and category B. For the purposes of description it is necessary to pretend that a cline is a scale with a number of discrete points, each of which can be explicitly specified. An item can then be assigned to a particular point on the scale so that its whereabouts can be more precisely stated.

All linguists are aware of the necessity of segmenting continua for the purposes of description, but they vary in the way in which they do this. Some linguists for the sake of simplicity cut up a continuum into the minimum number of segments

A | continu

B | um

and assign all items to one of the main categories, allowing no intermediate categories. For instance the continuum in the above diagram has been split into only two segments with a single cut-off point between them. Other linguists feel that to split a continuum into the minimum number of segments is to oversimplify. They prefer to split it into a larger number of segments. For instance the continuum in the diagram below has been split into four segments with three cut-off points.

More A	con
Less A	tin
Less B	uu
More B	m

Systemic linguists tend to prefer the more complex kind of segmenting, believing that it allows them to reflect more accurately in their descriptions the clines of their theory.

Systemic linguistics, then, considers that continua are sufficiently important to be represented in theoretical discussion. It is recognized that for the purposes of practical description continua must be segmented, but even here systemic linguistics keeps as close as possible to the clines of its theory by making the maximum rather than the minimum number of cuts in each continuum.

So far the discussion of clines has been rather abstract. Let me now give two examples—two important examples—of continua which transformational-generative grammarians prefer to segment using a single cut-off point (or do not discuss at all) but which systemic linguists would prefer to segment using a number of cut-off points.

First, there is the question of grammaticality. A transformational-generative grammar is concerned only with the grammatical sentences of a language. In fact a transformational-generative grammar is designed to distinguish between the grammatical sentences and the ungrammatical sentences.

(The TG concern with grammaticalness should not be confused with the traditional grammarians' concern with 'correctness' (1.2.1). As has been shown, discussions of 'correctness' are based on appeals to false authorities, whereas TG linguists define grammaticality in terms of acceptability to native speakers. A grammatical sentence is a sentence which would be accepted as well-formed by native speakers of the language under consideration. The TG concept of grammaticality does have some basis in reality.)

Grammaticality is a continuum. Some sentences of a language are quite clearly either acceptable or not acceptable to native speakers of the language. Very many sentences, however, would give rise to differences of opinion. Such sentences are marginally acceptable.

Transformational-generative linguists are well aware that grammaticality is a continuum but for practical purposes they assume a single cut-off point on the scale.

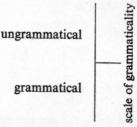

ungrammatical

grammatical

How does systemic linguistics differ from TG linguistics in respect of this question of grammaticality?

In the first place systemic linguistics would not define grammaticality in terms of acceptability, since the view of grammaticality as acceptability is akin to the view of *langue* as a form of 'knowing'. Systemic linguists would define grammaticality in terms more in line with their view of *langue* as a form of 'doing', in terms of the usualness of sentences, in terms of the likelihood of the sentences occurring.

In the second place systemic linguists would not want to discuss grammaticality without reference to the situation in which a sentence was being used. A sentence might well be unacceptable/unusual/unlikely in certain types of situation but acceptable/usual/likely in others.

In the third place, and this is the main point being made here, systemic linguists would not be happy with just a twofold segmentation of the scale. They would want at least three segments, preferably more, since this would allow them to come closer in practice to reflecting the cline which they recognize in theory.

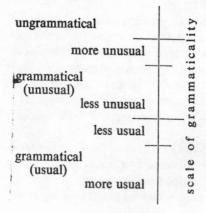

Through having a single cut-off point, TG linguists are forced to rule out as ungrammatical many of the sentences produced by literary writers. Systemic linguists are able to include such sentences under the heading of unusual (sometimes slightly unusual, sometimes very unusual) grammatical sentences. Transformational-generative linguists are well aware of the difficulty and a certain amount of discussion has gone on as to the best way of handling literary works within a TG frame of reference. Systemic linguists want to be able to handle literary works, the truly creative uses of language, within the main framework of their grammars.

The second continuum to be discussed here is the cline which systemic linguistics calls the *scale of delicacy*. Delicacy will be discussed more precisely in Chapter 9, but a few remarks will be made here since they are relevant to the general approach of systemic linguistics.

It was suggested earlier that the reason why some linguists preferred to cut up a continuum into the minimum number of segments was for the sake of simplicity. Certainly by preferring the more complex form of segmentation, systemic linguists do run the risk of not being able to see the wood for the trees. However to avoid this risk systemic linguists carry out their segmentation in stages, beginning by making the minimum number of cuts and then subdividing the segments and further subdividing them until they have reached the degree of segmentation which they require.

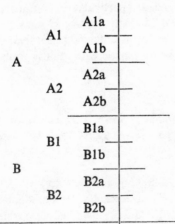

less delicate ←— scale of delicacy —→ more delicate

This enables the simpler minimal segmentation to be borne in mind while the more complex segmentation is being carried out.

The initial cut usually reflects the most obvious, or least delicate, distinction that can be made. The later cuts gradually reflect finer and finer, more and more delicate, distinctions. The more complex kinds of segmentation are related to the simpler kinds of segmentation on a cline which, as has been said, is called by systemic linguistics *the scale of delicacy*.

The inclusion of the concept of delicacy is one reason why the present writer enjoys teaching systemic linguistics. When teaching any particular aspect of language it is satisfying to be able to begin by introducing the class to the simplest, most obvious distinctions and then gradually to be able to lead them on through finer and finer distinctions to greater and greater complexities of language.

It should perhaps be reiterated that it is not being suggested that TG linguists are not aware of the clines which have been discussed here. (Certainly degrees of grammaticality have been discussed by TG linguists.) It is suggested that TG linguistics differs from systemic linguistics in two ways: in that TG linguists do not consider such clines sufficiently important to build them into their basic theory; and in that there is a tendency for TG in practice to make fewer cuts in clines than are made by systemic linguistics.

This distinguishing feature of systemic linguistics, the tendency to see things in terms of clines, is a direct result of the distinguishing feature discussed in 2.1.3, the tendency to show a greater interest in the less general forms of language, particular languages, particular varieties of language, particular idiolects, particular texts. The more interested one is in the less general forms of language for their own sake, the more prepared one has to be to grapple with infinite gradations and multiple complexities.

2.1.5 *Systemic Linguistics Seeks Verification of Its Hypotheses by Means of Observations from Texts and by Means of Statistical Techniques*

It has been said (1.2.3.3) that linguists seek objective verification of their hypotheses. In this, systemic linguists are like other linguists.

It was also indicated in 1.2.3.3 that there are different ways of verifying hypotheses and of otherwise validating statements about language. Some schools tend to prefer some ways, some others.

It is perhaps true to say that systemic linguists are more inclined than transformational-generative linguists to seek verification of their hypotheses by means of observations from collections of texts and by means of statistical techniques. (It is again important to stress that this is a *relative* question.)

It has already been said that systemic linguistics is interested in less general forms of language such as particular texts and particular idiolects, as well as in the more general forms. This interest in the less general forms often involves considering what particular people 'do' on particular occasions in the light of what they 'can do'. *Langue* is used to shed light on *parole*.

The point that is being made here is that the reverse is also true. *Parole* is used to shed light on *langue*. Hypotheses about what the people of a particular cultural group 'can do' linguistically can to a large extent be verified by observations of what they 'do do' in actual texts.

It is easier to use *parole* to shed light on *langue*, and vice versa, in systemic linguistics than in TG linguistics, since the relationship between the members of the systemic opposition 'does' v. 'can do' is much simpler than the extremely complex relationship between the members of the TG opposition 'does' v. 'knows'. 'Does' and 'knows' can only indirectly be used to shed light on each other.

As was shown in 2.1.4 systemic linguistics is also concerned with questions of usualness or likelihood of occurrence. It is interesting to consider what a person 'does' in a particular situation, not only in the light of what he 'can do' but also in the light of what he 'is likely to do', in that situation. It is in order to verify hypotheses about the relative likelihood of linguistic options that systemic linguists make use of statistical techniques.

2.1.6   Systemic Linguistics Has as Its Central Category the Category of the System

The term *system* will be explained fully in Chapter 8. It is being mentioned here because it is the distinguishing feature from which systemic linguistics takes its name.

When a school of linguistics has decided on its general approach, on its aims and priorities, it then has to decide on a form of model which will represent language in the way most suited to its purposes. Systemic linguistics represents language as a series of systems.

It was stated in 2.1.2 that systemic linguists view *langue* as linguistic behaviour potential, as the range of options from which a person's language and the culture to which he belongs allow him to select.

Each system is a set of these linguistic behavioural options, a set of options available in a certain specifiable environment.

The category of the system, then, is derived from the systemic view of *langue* as 'possibilities for doing'. It is directly relatable to the systemic interest in the sociological aspects of language. It provides a framework against the background of which systemic linguists can consider particular texts, particular idiolects; it is the 'can do' in the light of which one considers the 'does'.

It would perhaps be helpful at this point to summarize what has been said about the distinguishing features of systemic linguistics.

Systemic linguistics shows particular interest in the sociological aspects of language. As a result of this it views language as a form of 'doing' rather than as a form of 'knowing'. Systemic linguistics is interested in the less general as well as the more general forms of language. As a result of this it tends to explain aspects of language in terms of clines. When seeking verification of hypotheses about the more general forms of language, systemic linguistics turns to actual texts and to statistical techniques. Systemic linguistics has developed a model of language suited to its overall view of language and to the priorities it has established. The central category of this model is the system, a system being a set of linguistic options available in a certain environment.

2.2 THE AIMS, SCOPE AND ORGANIZATION OF THE PRESENT BOOK

Now that these introductory explanations have been made, a more precise account of the aims and scope of this book can be given than was possible in the preface. It can be shown what the book does attempt to do and what it only partially attempts to do or does not attempt to do at all.

First, what does it attempt to do? A fair amount of space has been given in the introductory chapters to the discussion of models, these models being contributory factors in the pursuit of such ideals as insightfulness, coherence, consistency, explicitness and objective verifiability. It has been stated that systemic linguistics makes use of models just as other schools of linguistics do. In 1.2.3.4 various kinds of model were distinguished, among these being the outline theoretical model. Each school of linguistics has its own outline theoretical model. This book attempts to present the outline theoretical model used by systemic linguistics.

Now, what does the book only partially attempt to do or not attempt to do at all? The book is by no means intended to be a complete account of systemic linguistics. As has been said, it does attempt to present the outline theoretical model of systemic linguistics but it does not present in full any of the detailed models within the main model (1.2.3.4). Some of these detailed models are sketched in, however, and reference is made at relevant points in the text to fuller accounts of them.

There are other ways, too, in which the book is far from being a complete account of systemic linguistics. Very little account is given of the history of systemic linguistics. Those readers interested in seeing how this kind of linguistics has developed are recommended to read the following: Firth, 1957; then Halliday, 1961 and Halliday *et al.*, 1964; and finally Halliday, 1971a, Hudson, 1971 and Halliday, forthcoming.

As has been said, there are differences of opinion within the school of systemic linguistics. Any introductory account of a subject must inevitably be selective. The views presented in this book are those with which the present writer happens to agree. For the most part these views are the views of Professor M. A. K. Halliday. At one or two points in the book, however, a line other than Professor Halliday's has been followed. Perhaps the most important of these points are the discussions of *depth* in Chapters 5 and 7, where the views adopted are those of Dr R. D. Huddleston. At one or two points the present writer has deliberately clung to views which the original authors of the views have now rejected, since she still considers the earlier approach to be of value.

Some attempt has been made to indicate the points at which there are differences of opinion. A complete account of such differences is, of course, beyond the scope of an introductory work. The aim has been simply to give a sense of perspective, to indicate that such differences exist, rather than to make a systematic study of the differences. To supplement the account of systemic linguistics given here, readers are advised to read Halliday, 1971a, Hudson, 1971 and Halliday, forthcoming.

It has been even more necessary to be selective when trying to give an account of linguistics in general and when trying to make comparisons between systemic linguistics and other schools. The present book does not assume any prior knowledge on the part of its readers of the work of other schools of linguistics. Consequently the comparisons between schools, in Section 1 of Chapter 2 and elsewhere in the book, have had to be made in the most general terms. A number of issues have had to be oversimplified and steps in the reasoning have had to be omitted. Those readers interested in more detailed discussions of some of the similarities and differences between systemic linguistics and TG linguistics are referred to Halliday, 1971a and Hudson, 1971.

To supplement the general account of linguistics given in Sections 1 and 2 of Chapter 1, the following are recommended: Crystal, 1968; Crystal, 1971; Lyons, 1970a; Lyons, 1970b. Crystal, 1971 is particularly recommended for its discussion of the scientificness of linguistics (Chapter 3).

No systematic account has been given in the present book of the contribution made or likely to be made by systemic linguistics to general linguistics, descriptive linguistics, contrastive linguistics or applied linguistics. However some attempt has been made to give some indication of this in a rather impressionistic way in the Discussion sections to be found at the ends of most chapters. Those readers who feel they would like to see something of the applications of systemic linguistics before proceeding further with this book are recommended to read Halliday, 1971b, Halliday, 1969, Bernstein, 1971 and 1972 (especially the papers by Turner and Hasan) and Doughty *et al.*, 1971.

The present book is not intended to be a description of English. Since the book is intended for students in English departments, a certain amount of description of English has been included—enough to enable students to discuss passages of English in an elementary way in the light of systemic linguistics—but the book is very far from being a complete description of the language. Systemic descriptions of English as such can be found in Sinclair, 1965 and 1972 and in Muir, 1972.

It should be noted that although most of the description in the present book is of English, systemic linguistics can be used in the description of any language. It has in fact been used in the description of languages which vary as greatly as French, Chinese and Nzema. Occasional references are made in this book to languages other than English.

It will perhaps be obvious from what has been said that the book has been written on two different levels of systematicness. The core of the book, the outline theoretical model of systemic linguistics, has, it is hoped, been dealt with fully and systematically. Other matters, such as the linguistic background of the model, the finer points of the model and the *raison d'être* of the model, have been dealt with less systematically, the aim being merely to give readers an impression of what lies beyond the boundaries of this book.

The book has also been written on different levels of complexity. In general the plan has been to begin each chapter by introducing the topic of the chapter in the simplest way possible and then gradually to introduce more and more complexities. For this reason most of the chapters become more difficult to read as they progress. Readers completely new to linguistics might find it useful initially just to read the first one or two sections of each chapter in order to gain an overall view of what the book is about, before returning to read the book as a whole.

Another way in which different levels of complexity have been introduced into the book is by means of passages in small print. These small print passages have been used for two main purposes.

Firstly, they have been used to provide additional explanation where the explanation in the main body of the text was not felt to be sufficient. Such additional explanation is often of a peripheral and sometimes of an informal and unscientific nature. These passages are designed to help readers who may be at a disadvantage owing to lack of familiarity with traditional grammar.

Secondly, they have been used to indicate alternative views or more advanced approaches to topics. The explanation in these cases is much more telescoped than that of the main body of the text and as a consequence it is probably less clear. As has been said, the intention has been merely to indicate that such alternative approaches exist rather than to fully explain them.

The small print passages in the early chapters are mainly for the first purpose, those in the later chapters mainly for the second.

Readers are advised to bear in mind while reading the book the attitudes to language and language study described in 1.2. They should particularly take note of the remarks made in 1.2.2.3. There is a danger that systemic linguistics, or any other kind of modern linguistics, may degenerate, like traditional grammar, into a process of labelling just for the sake of labelling, unless it is studied with some definite purpose in mind. Before going on to Chapter 3, readers are advised to select two or three passages of language which they would be interested in comparing. They might for instance select two or three poems on a similar theme. Or they might select passages which they would expect to show similarities or differences of register. At the end of each chapter they are advised to try to apply to their passages the concepts introduced in the chapter, with a view to seeing whether the concepts help them to pinpoint the similarities and differences in which they are interested.

Bibliographies, organized under chapter headings, will be found at the end of each volume. The bibliography of each chapter should be regarded as an integral part of the chapter. As indicated in the preface, the writer of the present book is very heavily indebted indeed to other writers. Chapter by chapter acknowledgements will be made in the bibliographies.

As has been said, the present book is in no way intended to be a complete course in systemic linguistics, still less a course in linguistics in general. The aim has been merely to familiarize readers with the basic ideas of systemic linguistics, so that they will be able to read with comparative ease the more advanced books on the subject. It is very necessary that readers should go on to read the more advanced books, in order to supplement the information given in this book and in order to counteract any distorted impressions which they may have received from this book as a result of the author's attempts to simplify the concepts for the sake of beginners.

3
Levels of Language

3.1 THE PRIMARY LEVELS OF LANGUAGE

The systemic model of language represents language as having three primary *levels*: substance, form and situation.

3.1.1 *Substance*

Substance is the raw material of language, the sounds that we use when we speak and the symbols that we use when we write.

3.1.2 *Form*

Form is the arrangement of the substance into recognizable and meaningful patterns.

D, t, y, o, a is simply an inventory of some of the letters that can be used to write English. In *today* these letters have been rearranged into a recognizable and meaningful English pattern. *D, t, y, o, a* has substance; *today* has both substance and form.

3.1.3 *Situation*

Situation is precisely what it sounds like, the situation in which a given bit of language is used.

Today has some sort of meaning, even if it is used quite out of the blue with no reference to anything in particular. But its meaning remains incomplete until it is used in a situation. If William the Conqueror had said *Today I have won the Battle of Hastings*, his *today* would have meant 14 October 1066. If the Duke of Wellington had said *Today I have won the Battle of Waterloo*, his *today* would have meant 18 June 1815. The meaning of a bit of language varies slightly according to the situation in which it is used.

3.2   THE SUBDIVISIONS OF THE PRIMARY LEVELS

Each of the three primary levels can be subdivided.

3.2.1   *The Subdivisions of Substance*

Substance can be divided into the substance of spoken language and the substance of written language. The substance of spoken language is called *phonic substance*. The substance of written language is called *graphic substance*.

3.2.2   *The Subdivisions of Form*

Form can be divided into lexis and grammar.

Lexis is concerned with individual items of language and the patterns in which individual items of language occur. In each of the sentences

Ex. 3.1   *John liked to play fair*
Ex. 3.2   *Peter was a lover of fair play*

the two individual items of language *play* and *fair* occur. In each sentence they occur in close proximity to each other. It is, in fact, part of the lexical patterning of English that *play* and *fair* frequently do occur together, unlike items such as *fish* and *metallurgy*, which are most unlikely to co-occur.

Grammar is concerned with classes of linguistic item and the patterns in which classes of linguistic item occur. In each of the two sentences cited above, Ex. 3.1 and Ex. 3.2 the first item is a proper name, while the second item is a verb. *John* and *Peter* belong to the same class of item; they are both proper names. *Liked* and *was* belong to the same class of item; they are both verbs. *John liked* has the same grammatical pattern as *Peter was*. This grammatical pattern, a member of the proper name class of items followed by a member of the verb class of items, is a very common one in English.

The two sentences, Ex. 3.1 and Ex. 3.2 are grammatically alike, then, as far as their first two words are concerned. And they are lexically alike as far as their last two words are concerned. They both begin with the classes proper name and verb, and they both end with the individual items *play* and *fair*.

However, their first two words, although grammatically alike, are lexically different. And their last two words, although lexically alike, are grammatically different.

John, although the same class of item as *Peter*, is a different individual item from *Peter*. *Liked*, although the same class of item as *was*, is a different individual item from *was*. Although *John liked* has the same classes of item as *Peter was* and is therefore grammatically the same as *Peter was*, *John liked* has no individual items in common with *Peter was* and is therefore lexically different from *Peter was*.

Play fair and *fair play*, on the other hand, have the individual items *fair* and *play* in common and are therefore lexically alike. They are grammatically different, however, since they consist of different classes of item; *play fair* consists of verb followed by adverb, while *fair play* consists of adjective followed by noun.

Other examples of pairs of stretches of language which have the same lexical pattern but different grammatical patterns are

Ex. 3.3   *The cat purred*
Ex. 3.4   *The purring cat*

and

Ex. 3.5   *The sun gleamed brightly*
Ex. 3.6   *The sun's bright gleam.*

Other examples of pairs of stretches of language which have the same grammatical pattern but different lexical patterns are

Ex. 3.7   *The cat purred*
Ex. 3.8   *The dog barked*

and

Ex. 3.9   *The white snow*
Ex. 3.10   *The green grass.*

3.2.3 *The Subdivisions of Situation*

Situation has no subdivisions which are as obvious or as generally accepted as those of substance and form. However, I shall mention one set of subdivisions which have been suggested for situation, as I think this particular set helps to convey an impression of the range of things which can be included under the heading of situation.

It has been suggested that situation should be divided into thesis, immediate situation and wider situation (Ellis, 1966).

The *thesis* of an utterance is what is being talked about.

The thesis of the utterance

Ex. 3.11   *A wasp has just flown in at that window*

includes and and the action of flying.

The *immediate situation* is precisely what it sounds like, the situation in which an utterance is actually used. I have on many occasions used the utterance Ex. 3.11 in lectures in order to exemplify the subdivisions of situation. On each of these occasions the immediate situation of the utterance consisted of myself talking to a class of students with the purpose of explaining a linguistic concept.

The *wider situation* of an utterance includes anything in the past experience of the speaker or writer which leads him to choose the particular utterance and to formulate it in the way that he does.

When I used the utterance Ex. 3.11 in lectures, my past experience included the fact that previous lectures in the series had been interrupted by wasps flying in through windows and distracting my audience. (The particular series of lectures in question was usually given at the beginning of the autumn term in low buildings whose windows opened on to a row of shrubs and bushes.) I chose the utterance because it was topical.

The wider situation of an utterance also includes anything in the past experience of the hearer or reader which leads him to interpret the utterance in the way that he does. Like myself, my classes had had experience of wasps interrupting lectures. This enabled them to interpret my utterance as a topical allusion.

My classes understood the wasp sentence in three different ways, each way being related to their knowledge of one of the kinds of situation. They knew what the thesis of the utterance was and they understood that I wanted them to think of a wasp flying in through a window.

However they realized from their knowledge of the immediate situation that the most important information I was trying to communicate to them via the sentence about the wasp was not information about a wasp, but information about the linguistic concept of situation. From their knowledge of the wider situation they understood that the utterance was a topical allusion.

3.3 THE INTERLEVELS OF LANGUAGE

In addition to the three primary levels of language, there are *interlevels* which link the primary levels together.

3.3.1 *Context*

The interlevel which links form and situation is called *context*.

Being an interlevel, context is concerned, not with entities (in the way in which substance is concerned with sounds and symbols, form with items, classes and patterns, situation with elements of situation), but rather with relationships between entities. Context is concerned with the relationships between the entities of form, the items, classes and patterns, on the one hand, and the entities of situation, the elements of situation, on the other.

For instance, context is concerned with the relationships between the individual linguistic items of lexis and elements of thesis. It is concerned, for example, with the relationship between the linguistic item *wasp* and the element of thesis , the relationship between the linguistic item *window* and the element of thesis , the relationship between the linguistic item *pin* and the element of thesis , the relationship between the linguistic item *cat* and the element of thesis . This kind of relationship, the relationship between a linguistic item and an element of thesis, is what most people mean by the term *meaning*. The meaning of an item is its relationship with an element of thesis.

Sometimes the relationship is more complicated than those in the examples already given. The linguistic item *waspish* has a relationship not only with the element of thesis but also with a person who is thought to have some of the qualities of a wasp.

Context is also concerned with the relationships between the individual linguistic items of lexis and elements of immediate situation. The items *cigarette* and *fag* can both be related to the same element of thesis ✏. But they can be related to different kinds of immediate situation. The item *fag* might be used by someone chatting to a group of friends in a pub. The item *cigarette* might be used by someone at a formal dinner-party sitting next to his ex-headmaster. The item *fag* can be related to an element of informality in the immediate situation. The item *cigarette* can be related to an element of formality in the immediate situation.

There are also relationships between individual linguistic items and elements of wider situation. Two Nottingham students once spent about ten minutes hunting for some *daps* without knowing what they were looking for. Another student had said that she had lost her daps and her friends were anxious to be helpful, but did not like to confess that they had never heard the word *daps* before. The loser of the daps had used the term *daps* because her wider situation included the fact that she came from Somerset, where *daps* is the name given to gym shoes. Her friends' wider situation did not include an element of Somerset-ness and they were unable to interpret the item.

So far all the examples given of contextual relationships have been between elements of situation and the individual linguistic items of lexis. Context is also concerned with relationships between elements of situation and the classes and patterns of grammar.

There are relationships between grammar and elements of thesis. It is possible to say, for instance, that each grammatical class can be related to an element of thesis.

A member of the verb class of items can usually be related to an element of thesis which we might label 'action' or 'process'. In the examples

Ex. 3.12   *The wasp buzzed*
Ex. 3.13   *The window broke*
Ex. 3.14   *The pin pricked*
Ex. 3.15   *The cat mewed*

the items *buzzed, broke, pricked, mewed* all have something in common in their meaning. They all denote some kind of action or process.

A member of the noun class of items can usually be related to an element of thesis which we might label 'participant in process'. The items *wasp, window, pin, cat* all have something in common in their meaning. They all denote something which can participate in a process.

In each of the sentences

Ex. 3.16   *The rebel worked hard*
Ex. 3.17   *The hard worker rebelled*

the item *rebel* occurs. It is the same lexical item, the same individual linguistic item, in both sentences. In both sentences it can be related to the same element of thesis, an element of thesis which we might define as 'opposition to authority'.

However, the item belongs to different grammatical classes in the two sentences. In the first sentence it is a noun, in the second sentence a verb. Although lexically it can be related to the same element of thesis in the two sentences, grammatically it can be related to different elements of thesis. In the first sentence it can be related to the element of thesis 'participant in process'. In the second sentence it can be related to the element of thesis 'process'.

The total meaning of an item is a combination of its lexical meaning and its grammatical meaning. *Rebel* in sentence Ex. 3.16 and *rebel* in sentence Ex. 3.17 have partially the same meaning since they are lexically alike, but they do not have the same total meaning since they are grammatically different.

Context is also concerned with relationships between grammar and elements of immediate situation. The two sentences

Ex. 3.18   *Close the door*
Ex. 3.19   *Would you close the door*

can be said to have the same thesis. But they can be related to different kinds of immediate situation. The first sentence would probably be used either in an immediate situation in which people were being rude to each other or in an immediate situation in which people were so well known to each other that there was no need for elaborate forms of politeness. The second sentence would probably be used in an immediate situation in which people were being polite to each other, not knowing each other well enough to dispense with such forms of politeness.

The two sentences have different grammatical patterns. The first sentence has the pattern of a direct command. The second sentence, although not in fact a question, has the grammatical pattern usually associated with a question.

The grammatical pattern of the first sentence can be related to an element of impoliteness or an element of familiarity in the immediate situation. The grammatical pattern of the second sentence can be related to elements of politeness and unfamiliarity in the immediate situation.

There are also relationships between grammar and elements of wider situation. For instance, the grammatical pattern of

Ex. 3.20   *She's clever is Susan*

would probably be used only by someone from the North of England. Speakers from other parts of the country would be more likely to say *She's clever, Susan is* or simply *Susan's clever*. The grammatical pattern of sentence Ex. 3.20 can be related to an element of northernness in the wider situation of a speaker.

It is important to realize that *context* here has a different meaning from the meaning it has when used in literary or everyday language. It is perhaps a bad term to use for the interlevel, as it causes confusion among those who are already familiar with the more usual meaning of *context*. Other names have been suggested for the interlevel. *Plerology*, a new term, has been invented especially for the purpose,[1] and it has also been suggested that *ecology* should be borrowed from the sciences.[2] Ecology, in the biological sciences, is the study of the mutual relations between organisms and their environment; if borrowed into linguistics, it would be the study of mutual relations between the items, classes and patterns of linguistic form and their situation. Neither plerology nor ecology has yet found general acceptance in systemic linguistics and, regrettably, *context* is still the term used for the interlevel which deals with the relationships between form and situation.

3.3.2 *Phonology and Graphology*

There are two interlevels which link form and substance: phonology and graphology.

Phonology links form and phonic substance. It is concerned with the relationships between distinctions in form and differences in sound.

For instance it is concerned with the relationships between grammatical patterns and the intonation patterns, the pitch movements, that we use when we speak. The sentences

Ex. 3.21   *You're coming with us*
Ex. 3.22   *Are you coming with us?*

---

[1] By Professor J. C. Catford in a talk given to the Linguistics Association of Great Britain, May 1962
[2] By Mr H. M. P. Davies, in conversation

have different grammatical patterns. The grammatical pattern of Ex. 3.21 is usually (though not invariably) associated with a falling intonation pattern. The grammatical pattern of Ex. 3.22 is usually (though not invariably) associated with a rising intonation pattern.

Phonology is also concerned with relationships between grammar and stress patterns. The item *record* occurs in both the following examples:

Ex. 3.23   *The record of the concert*
Ex. 3.24   *He is going to record the concert.*

It is the same lexical item in both examples but, whereas in Ex. 3.23 it is grammatically a member of the noun class of items, in Ex. 3.24 it is grammatically a member of the verb class of items. The difference in grammatical class is reflected in the difference in stress pattern. *Record* in Ex. 3.23 has its first syllable stressed, while *record* in Ex. 3.24 has its second syllable stressed. Other examples of items which similarly vary their stress pattern according to their grammatical class include *produce, progress, conduct.*

Phonology is also concerned with relationships between lexical distinctions and differences in sound. *Bin, din, fin, gin, kin, Min* (short for Minnie), *pin, sin, tin, win* are all different lexical items. We know they are different when we hear them since each begins with a different sound.

Graphology links form and graphic substance. It is concerned with the relationships between distinctions in form and differences in written symbols.

For instance it is concerned with the relationships between grammatical patterns and punctuation marks. The sentences

Ex. 3.21   *You're coming with us.*
Ex. 3.22   *Are you coming with us?*

have different grammatical patterns and, as we have seen, in spoken language the different grammatical patterns are usually associated with different intonation patterns. In written language the different grammatical patterns are usually (though again not invariably) associated with different punctuation marks, the grammatical pattern of Ex. 3.21 being associated with a full stop and the grammatical pattern of Ex. 3.22 being associated with a question mark.

Like phonology, graphology can sometimes distinguish between a lexical item acting as a member of one grammatical class and the same lexical item acting as a member of a different grammatical class. In

Ex. 3.25   *The prophecy was accurate*
Ex. 3.26   *He was able to prophesy accurately*

we find two different spellings of the lexical item *prophecy/prophesy*. The *c* spelling in Ex. 3.25 indicates that grammatically the item is acting as a member of the noun class of items. The *s* spelling in Ex. 3.26 indicates that grammatically the item is acting as a member of the verb class of items. Other examples of items spelt with a *c* when they are nouns and with an *s* when they are verbs include *practice/practise, device/devise*.

Graphology, like phonology, can distinguish between different lexical items. In spoken English we recognize that *bin, din, fin, gin, kin, Min, pin, sin, tin, win* are all different lexical items since each begins with a different sound. In written English we recognize them as different lexical items since each begins with a different letter.

3.4   LEVELS OF LANGUAGE AND BRANCHES OF LINGUISTICS

The terms *phonology, graphology, grammar, lexis, context*, as used in this chapter, each have two meanings. The levels are first and foremost levels of language. But each level of language has a branch of linguistics which is devoted to the study of that particular level. The name of the level of language is usually used also for the branch of linguistics which studies the level. *Context* means both the set of relationships between bits of linguistic form and their situations and also the branch of linguistics which studies these relationships. *Lexis* means both the set of individual linguistic items and their patterns and also the branch of linguistics which studies these items and patterns. *Grammar, phonology* and *graphology* are each used with a similar pair of meanings.

The term *grammar* can also be used with a wider pair of meanings than those indicated for it in this chapter. It can be used to include phonology, graphology, lexis and context as well as the level of language which has been called *grammar* in this chapter. And it can be used to include all the corresponding branches of linguistics—phonology, graphology, lexis and context—as well as the branch of linguistics which has been called *grammar* in this chapter. Thus, in the second of this wider pair of meanings, the term *grammar* is virtually synonymous with the term *linguistics* and can on occasion be used interchangeably with it. For instance an alternative title for this book would have been *An Introduction to Systemic Grammar*. The book would still have included discussion of phonology, graphology, lexis and context as well as discussion of grammar in the narrower sense. However in order to avoid confusion between the narrower and the wider meanings, the term *grammar* will always be used in this book with one of the narrower meanings, while the terms *language* and *linguistics* will be used for the wider meanings.

The correspondence between the levels of language and the branches of linguistics can perhaps best be shown diagrammatically. Figure 3.1 shows the levels of language. Figure 3.2 shows the branches of linguistics.

FIGURE 3.1   *The Levels of Language*

SUBSTANCE	←——→	FORM	←——→	SITUATION
phonic substance graphic substance	phonology graphology	grammar lexis	context	thesis immediate situation wider situation

FIGURE 3.2   *The Branches of Linguistics*

PHONETICS/ GRAPHETICS	LINGUISTICS			OTHER SUBJECTS
	phonology graphology	grammar lexis	context	

It will be seen from the diagrams that the main area of correspondence is the central area covering phonology, graphology, grammar, lexis and context.

Linguistics is concerned with the two levels of form, grammar and lexis, and with the interlevels, context, phonology and graphology. It has a branch for each of these levels.

Linguistics is not concerned with situation as such, only with the relationships between situation and form. It thus includes context but excludes situation.

Nor is linguistics concerned with phonic or graphic substance as such, only with the ways in which phonic and graphic substance are made use of in linguistic form. It thus includes phonology and graphology but excludes substance.

On each side of Figure 3.2, linguistics can be seen to overlap with other subjects.

On the left it overlaps with *phonetics* and *graphetics*. Phonetics and graphetics, like linguistics, are interested in the ways in which substance is made use of in linguistic form; they overlap with linguistics in phonology and graphology. Unlike linguistics, however, phonetics and graphetics are also interested in substance for its own sake regardless of if or how it is made use of in linguistic form. Phonetics and graphetics are not concerned with grammar, lexis, context or situation. Phonetics and linguistics together are known as the *linguistic sciences*. Strictly speaking, graphetics should be included in the linguistic sciences too but, although in theory there is a subject called *graphetics*, in practice very little attention has so far been paid to it.

On the other side of the diagram linguistics overlaps with all other academic subjects. All other subjects study some aspect of situation, and all other subjects are interested in the relationships between their particular concepts and the bits of linguistic form which express these concepts.

Professor J. R. Firth (Firth, 1957) likened the levels of language to the colours of the rainbow. The analysis of language into its levels is like an experiment with white light. One sees a beam of light, holds up a prism, converts the white light into the colours of the spectrum, holds up another prism, converts the spectrum back into white light, and looks again at the beam of light with a new awareness of the colours that go to make it up. One reads or hears a piece of language, analyses it into levels, then re-reads or re-hears the language with a new awareness of its composition.

The spectrum analogy will perhaps prevent us from being misled by the diagrams into thinking of the levels of language as too rigidly distinct from each other. They sometimes seem to shade into each other as do the colours of the rainbow.

3.5 DISCUSSION

It is a little early as yet in the explanation of the systemic model of language to demonstrate its relevance to general, descriptive, contrastive and applied linguistics. It will be appreciated that at this elementary stage it is not possible to make any very penetrating or sophisticated statements on these matters. If we could say all we wanted to say about language and language study after one chapter's worth of systemic linguistics, there would be no point in going any further. A few points may be made, however.

3.5.1 General Linguistics

The concept of level of language is the first stage in systemic linguists' attempts to answer the questions posed by general linguistics. What is language? Language is something which consists of different levels: substance, form, situation. How does language work? Language works through these different levels and through the way in which the levels are related to each other, the relationships between the levels being the concern of the interlevels. (The way in which the levels are related to each other will be further discussed in Volume II, as will the levels themselves.) What have all languages got in common? All languages consist of different levels: all languages have substance; all languages have form; all languages have situation.

3.5.2 Descriptive and Contrastive Linguistics

When describing and contrasting particular languages or varieties of a language, we can use the levels of language as a framework for our descriptions. The framework will suggest questions that we should ask ourselves which will help us to achieve a comprehensive description and which, in a comparison, will help us to pinpoint the areas in which the similarities and differences are to be found. It is very important when engaged on any kind of academic study to know what questions to ask.

No matter what languages or varieties of a language we are comparing we shall find that, as indicated above, they are all similar in that they consist of substance, form and situation. We shall further find that they are similar in that their form can be subdivided into grammar and lexis. We shall probably find, however, that they differ in particular details of their grammar and in particular details of their lexis. We might well ask ourselves: Are the differences in the details of the grammar greater than the differences in the lexis, or vice versa?

We shall find, too, that the languages or varieties of a language are similar in that their situation can be divided into thesis, immediate situation and wider situation, but again we shall probably find that the details differ. We shall find that the differences in detail of form are relatable via context to the differences in detail of situation. We might well ask ourselves, particularly if we are comparing different registers: How far are the differences in form occasioned by the differences in the subject matter, the thesis? How far are the differences in form occasioned by the differences in the immediate situation? How far are the differences in form occasioned by the differences in the wider situation of the participants?

Whereas for all languages and varieties of a language it is true that form can be subdivided into grammar and lexis and that situation can be subdivided into thesis, immediate situation and wider situation, it is not true for all languages that substance can be divided into phonic substance and graphic substance. Any language that has no written version will have no graphic substance, only phonic substance. Such languages will have no interlevel of graphology, only phonology. Thus a more basic difference is possible between languages in respect of their substance than in respect of their form and situation. Even among those languages which have both phonic and graphic substance, it is possible for basic differences to be found. Both English and Chinese have both phonic and graphic substance, but the relationship between graphic substance and form for English is very different from the relationship between graphic substance and form for Chinese. (This difference between English and Chinese will be discussed in Volume II Chapter 5.) Those languages which have both phonic and graphic substance and which relate their graphic substance to form in the same way as English may still differ from English in matters of detail of phonic and graphic substance.

3.5.3 Systemic Linguistics and Other Schools of Linguistics

Most models of language include the concept of level of language, though they do not all use the same term for this concept and they do not all recognize the same number of levels. The most noteworthy difference between the systemic model and other models is the importance which the systemic model attaches to the interlevel of context. Whereas other schools of linguistics show interest in the relationships between form and thesis, most other schools do not, at any rate to the same extent, show interest in the relationships between form and immediate situation or in the relationships between form and wider situation. This concern of systemic linguistics for the interlevel of context is part of its interest in the sociological aspects of language (2.1.1).

4
Chain and Choice

4.1 CHAIN (THE SYNTAGMATIC AXIS)

Any utterance consists of a number of bits of language, one after another, in a sequence, the sequence being one-dimensional like a line. The dimension along which the sequence occurs is called the dimension or axis of *chain*. Each bit of language forms a link in the whole chain of a complete utterance.

When we are considering spoken language, we can regard the dimension of chain as a time dimension. The bits of language occur one after another in time. When we are considering written language, we can regard the dimension of chain as either a time dimension or a space dimension. We write the bits of language one after another in time and we read them one after another in time. We can also regard written language as existing in space, whether we read it or not. In this case the bits of language occur one after another in space along the lines of a page.

A more technical name which is sometimes given to the axis of chain is the *syntagmatic axis*.

4.2 PATTERNS

Patterns occur along the dimension of chain.

Each language has a number of patterns which belong to it but does not have certain others. For instance, English has the phonological and graphological patterns which we find in *pin, bin, tin, din,* but does not have the patterns in *pni, bni, tni, dni.* English also has the grammatical pattern which we find in *the red book, the old man,* but does not have the pattern in *book red the, man old the.* English has the lexical pattern

which we find in *bright red dress*, but does not have the pattern in
invisible red thunder; it has the lexical pattern which we find in *the cat
purred contentedly*, but not the pattern in *the dog purred unhappily*. All
these patterns are composed of bits of language which occur one after
another along the axis of chain.

4.3   CHOICE (THE PARADIGMATIC AXIS)

At each point in a pattern there is a possibility of choice.

If we take the English pattern *-in*, we can fill the blank space with any
one of a number of possible choices. *Bin, din, fin, gin, kin, Min* (short for
Minnie), *pin, sin, tin, win* are all possible in English. If we take the
English pattern *p-n*, we can choose *a, e, i* or *u* to fill the space. The space
in *pi-* can be filled by *g, n, p* or *t*.

The choices exemplified in the last paragraph are all phonological
and graphological choices. Choices can also be made at other levels of
language. If *I began* is chosen instead of *I have begun*, a grammatical
choice has been made. If *strange old fellow* is chosen instead of *strange
old man*, a lexical choice has been made.

We can arrange a pattern and its choices diagrammatically.

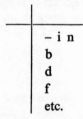

The basic pattern is shown along the horizontal axis, the axis of chain.
The possible choices are shown along the vertical axis, the axis of *choice*.

A more technical name for the axis of choice is the *paradigmatic
axis*.

It is important to realize that the term *choice* in this connection does
not necessarily imply conscious choice and does not necessarily imply
free choice.

The degree of consciousness of choice can range from completely,
or almost completely, subconscious choice to fully and explicitly conscious choice.

Someone talking about the element of thesis ⟋ will usually choose
to say *pin* rather than *bin*, but will usually not be aware of having
made any choice since the choice will have been made subconsciously.

On the other hand, the original author of *Peter Piper picked a peck of pickled pepper* must presumably have been fully conscious of his choice of *p* sounds. He would have been able to be explicit about the kind of choice he was making, probably using the term *alliteration* to refer to it, and he would have been able to be explicit about his reasons for making the choice, probably using the term *tongue-twister* to refer to what he was trying to achieve.

Between these two extremes, subconsciousness and full and explicit consciousness, are varying degrees of semi-consciousness. In Act I Scene i of *King Lear*, one of the ways in which Shakespeare contrasts Cordelia's speech with the speeches of her sisters is by giving some of her lines a predominance of verbs; he chooses a member of the verb class of items an unusually high number of times per line.

Ex. 4.1   *You have begot me, bred me, lov'd me: I*
Return those duties back as are right fit,
Obey you, love you, and most honour you.

Of course it is conceivable that Shakespeare's choices here were fully conscious. He may have explicitly formulated to himself the kind of choice he was making and his reasons for making it. (A predominance of verbs makes a speaker seem more sincere and down-to-earth, the sort of person who believes that actions speak louder than words? The repetition of the verb + object pattern chops up the rhythm, making it evident that Cordelia cannot heave her heart into her mouth, unlike her sisters who speak easily and fluently?) Or, perhaps more likely, Shakespeare's choices were semi-conscious. He may have been aware of a wish to distinguish Cordelia's language from that of her sisters and a wish to choose language which would be appropriate to her character, and he may have felt for the right choices, without necessarily being aware that his verbs were verbs and without explicitly labelling them as such.

What matters in linguistics (and in literary criticism?) is what choices are made, not how consciously they are made. It does not matter whether Shakespeare's choices of verbs were made fully consciously or only semi-consciously. What is important is that he did make those choices. From a linguistic point of view all choices are choices even if some are more conscious than others.

The degree of freedom of choice also seems, at any rate at first sight, to range very widely.

On the one hand there are choices which appear to be fully

determined by the situation in which they occur. If one is talking about the element of thesis ⟋, the very fact that one is talking about the element of thesis ⟋ will usually determine one's choice of *pin* rather than *bin*.

On the other hand there are choices which appear to be completely free. It may not seem to make much difference whether one says

Ex. 4.2 *Authority I respect but authoritarianism I deplore*

or

Ex. 4.3 *I respect authority but I deplore authoritarianism.*

However, I am acquainted with at least one person who frequently says *bin* when he means *pin* and *din* when he means *tin* because this is his idea of what is funny. So presumably we cannot say that even this kind of choice is fully determined by the situation.

And, given that one wishes to achieve a particular shade of emphasis and is in the kind of situation in which a rather rhetorical way of speaking is appropriate, one would be more likely to choose Ex. 4.2 than Ex. 4.3. So we cannot say that even this kind of choice is completely free and fully independent of its situation.

Again it is true to say that all choices are choices even if some appear to be freer than others.

4.4 CONTRASTS

Associated with the axis of chain is the concept of pattern. Associated with the axis of choice is the concept of contrast.

The possible choices that can fill a place in a pattern differ from each other. By being different, they signal differences in meaning; they are able to refer to different situations. The four English sentences

Ex. 4.4 *The pin is over there*
Ex. 4.5 *The bin is over there*
Ex. 4.6 *The tin is over there*
Ex. 4.7 *The din is over there*

have the same patterns. At one point in one of the patterns, different choices are made. As a result, the sentences have different meanings; they refer to different situations.

We speak of these meaningfully different choices as *contrasts*.

The contrasts exemplified in Ex. 4.4–7 are phonological and graphological contrasts. The sentences

Ex. 4.8   *The pin is over there*
Ex. 4.9   *The pin was over there*
Ex. 4.10 *The pin will be over there*

show grammatical contrasts. The sentences

Ex. 4.11 *The new pin is over there*
Ex. 4.12 *The rusty pin is over there*
Ex. 4.13 *The shiny pin is over there*

show lexical contrasts. In each case the contrasts signal differences in the situations referred to.

It is important to notice that these contrasts, the meaningfully different choices, are choices between things which can occupy the same place in the same pattern. It is not enough for bits of language just to be different. To be meaningfully different, to be contrasts, the bits of language must be capable of occurring in the same environment.

The sound which in English is spelt *ng* is different from the *p, b, t* and *d* sounds of examples Ex. 4.4–7. But it cannot be said to contrast with them since it can never in English occur, as they do, at the beginning of a word. There is no lexical item in English which is differentiated from *pin, bin, tin, din* by the fact that it begins with *ng*. No difference in situation can be signalled by the difference between *ng* and the *p, b, t, d* sounds of *pin, bin, tin, din*. It is not meaningfully different from them. It does not contrast with them.

In the lexical items *lip, lib* (as in *women's lib*), *lit, lid*, however, we find different versions of the *p, b, t, d* sounds. (The *p* in *lip* is a slightly different sound from the *p* in *pin* even though it sounds the same to most English ears. Similarly the *b* in *lib* is slightly different from the *b* in *bin*, the *t* in *lit* from the *t* in *tin*, and the *d* in *lid* from the *d* in *din*.) *Ng* does contrast with these versions of *p, b, t, d* since it can occur in the same place in the same phonological pattern. The lexical item *ling* is differentiated from *lip, lib, lit, lid* by the difference between *ng* and the *p, b, t, d* sounds. By distinguishing between different lexical items these sounds can signal differences in situation. They are meaningfully different.

In any given bit of language the choices which are present in particular positions will be contrasting with all the choices which might have been present in those positions but which are absent from that particular bit of language. The things which might have been present but which are absent are just as important in language as the things which are actually present. They do just as much towards enabling us to communicate.

If we use the item *pin*, as in Ex. 4.4, we are using a distinct lexical item in order to refer to a distinct element of thesis. Our hearers recognize the item and know that it is a different item from all the items we have not used, such as *bin* or *tin*, or *pen* or *pan*, or *pit* or *pig*. They know that it refers to a different element of thesis from any of these other items. They are able to recognize the item as a distinct lexical item because they know that the sounds which represent it are different from the sounds which represent the other lexical items. (If they are native speakers of English they know all this, subconsciously if not consciously, even if other examples such as Ex. 4.5–7 do not occur immediately next to Ex. 4.4 giving opportunity for comparison.)

If the *p*, *i* and *n* sounds did not contrast with anything else, we should not recognize them as distinct sounds. (This is why we do not recognize the *p* sounds in *pin* and *lip* as different sounds—because they do not contrast with each other.) They would not then be able to represent a distinct lexical item and we should not be able to refer to a distinct element of thesis.

If it were not for its contrasts, language would not be able to work at all. Individual items of language can only function because they are part of the system of contrasts of their language as a whole. It is the things with which they contrast which give them their ability to communicate.

We can say that the syntagmatic axis, the axis of chain, is the axis which links together the things that are present in a given bit of language, while the paradigmatic axis, the axis of choice, is the axis which links the things that are present to the things that are absent, the things with which they contrast.

4.5   DISCUSSION

4.5.1   *General Linguistics*

Like the concept of level of language, the concepts of chain and choice and the associated concepts of pattern and contrast help to explain what language is and how language works. Language is something which occurs sequentially along the axis of chain. It is patterned, the patterns occurring at all levels of language. At each point in each pattern different choices are possible. Language works through the way in which these different choices contrast with each other, signalling differences in situations. All languages have patterns along the axis of chain. All languages work by means of contrasting choices.

4.5.2 Descriptive and Contrastive Linguistics

When describing and contrasting particular languages or varieties of language we need to state what particular patterns are found in each language or variety of language and what contrasting choices are available at each point in each pattern.

When contrasting different registers we find that some registers make use of extra kinds of pattern and contrast in addition to the kinds which they have in common with other registers of their language. Literary language and advertising language, for instance, make use of the patterns which Professor J. McH. Sinclair has termed *latent patterns*.[1]

If we consider the line

Ex. 4.14 *Full fathom five thy father lies*

we find that it has a number of the patterns which all varieties of English have in common. *Five*, for instance, has a pattern of sounds which is quite usual in all registers of English. The line also has patterns of sounds which are not found in all other varieties of the language. For instance, four of the six words begin with *f*, making an alliterative pattern. Alliteration is a sound pattern which is not found in all registers of English. In most situations we try to avoid using alliteration. Literary language and advertising language, on the other hand, often make great use of it. Alliteration is a latent pattern, a pattern which is possible in the language, which is lying waiting to be used, but which will be avoided in certain situations, exploited in others.

Similarly, if we consider again the lines from *King Lear* given in Ex. 4.1, we find they contain a number of patterns which all registers of English have in common. For instance the grammatical pattern verb + object found in *obey you*, is a very common grammatical pattern found in all varieties of English. What is not so usual in all registers of the language is the repetition of this pattern three times in the space of eight words. The repetition is a latent pattern. This grammatical latent pattern, like the phonological latent pattern of alliteration, results from the same choice, the same quite usual choice, being made an unusually

In a talk given to the Hull Linguistic Circle, February 1963

high number of times in a small stretch of language. In the lines from
Lear the common grammatical pattern verb + object has been chosen
an unusually high number of times. In Ex. 4.14 the common English
sound *f* has been chosen an unusually high number of times. This is
how latent patterns usually are achieved, by making the same usual
choice unusually frequently.

4.5.3 *Applied Linguistics*

The recognition of latent patterns and contrasts is relevant to stylistics,
the kind of applied linguistics which links linguistics and literary studies.

Dylan Thomas, in *Fern Hill*, makes a great deal of use of latent patterns and contrasts. He wishes to draw attention to various things and
ideas connected with the central thought of the poem. He does this partly
by simply repeating certain lexical items such as *young*, *happy*, *green*,
time, *golden*, *sun*, *play*, *moon*, *born*. There are in fact comparatively few
lexical items in the poem which are used only once.

However, he does not repeat the lexical items haphazardly; he repeats
them in patterns, and the patterns help to draw attention to the things
he wishes to emphasize.

> *Time let me hail and climb*
> *Golden in the heydays of his eyes*
>
> *Time let me play and be*
> *Golden in the mercy of his means*

The repetition of the lexical items is here reinforced by the repetition of
the grammatical patterns and by the repetition of the phonological
patterns. Of the phonological patterns it is perhaps the rhythm which
most serves to give prominence to the repeated lexical items.
In the lines

> *Down the rivers of the windfall light*
>
> *In the pebbles of the holy streams*

the repetition of the water imagery is reflected in the grammatical similarity between the two lines. And, again, the fact that they occur in the
same position in their respective stanzas gives them a certain phonological similarity.

The poet is directing the attention of his reader or hearer by repetition and patterning at all levels of language. In fact the texture of the poem as a whole is rich with little intricately woven patterns.

Dylan Thomas also uses contrasts to mark the recurrent themes of the poem.

> *All the sun long*

> *All the moon long*

sun and *moon*, two of the significant lexical items in the poem, are here contrasting with each other. We might find these two items contrasting with each other in any kind of English. Dylan Thomas has used them in such a way as to introduce another kind of contrast in addition to the ordinary kind. He has used a pattern, *all the —— long*, which is perfectly familiar in everyday English, but he has substituted, for the choices which normally fit into the pattern, choices which we do not expect. We should expect *day, night, year* rather than *sun, moon*. The contrast between the usualness of the absent choices and the unusualness of the present choices draws attention to the important lexical items.

We find a similar contrast between absent and present elsewhere in the poem. For example

> *once below a time*

> *happy as the grass was green*

> *happy as the heart was long.*

An understanding of the last two of these and of the normal idiom with which they contrast makes it possible for us to understand

> *singing as the farm was home.*

There is, of course, pattern in the kind of contrast which Dylan Thomas employs in the poem. He is playing all the time with idioms which have something in common, and the something in common which they have is closely related to the central ideas of the poem.

Even more interesting is the way in which Dylan Thomas uses pattern and contrast to mark the relationship between the last two stanzas and the rest of the poem.

We find that in the last two stanzas earlier linguistic items and patterns are picked up and repeated: *foxes, house, happy, sun, hay, sky, tuneful, green, golden, moon, ride, sleep, fly, farm,* and *honoured among, happy as the heart was long, in the sun, as I was young and easy, in the mercy of his means, time held me green and dying.* In all of these some pattern or actual item from the earlier part of the poem is being repeated.

Yet in spite of all these links with the rest of the poem, the last two stanzas are set apart by contrasts at all levels of language.

At the level of graphology, the poet has established a pattern in which a full stop occurs at the end of each stanza. But between the last two stanzas there is just a comma. Out of the impressions of the first four stanzas has developed the central thought of the poem. There is more continuity between the last two stanzas than between the other stanzas. The thought is now more connected and less impressionistic.

This graphological contrast would be reflected in the phonology if the poem were read aloud.

At the level of grammar, a very important choice in language is that between positive and negative. It is significant that in this poem the only negative forms occur in the last two stanzas:

nothing I cared

Nothing I cared

Nor

We also find in the last two stanzas *heedless, few, childless,* which are sometimes described as negatives or virtual negatives.

In the last-but-one line of the poem a new and highly significant lexical item is introduced: *dying*. It occurs in the pattern *green and* ——, where earlier in the poem the choices *carefree* and *golden* were used. Unlike most of the lexical items, *dying* is used only once in the poem.

These differences in form of course reflect changes in the situation of the poem. In the first part of the poem, the poet is recapturing his earlier impressions. In the last two stanzas he is adding to these impressions a point-of-view which he has gained more recently. By repeating the patterns of the earlier part of the poem and by introducing significant new contrasting items, the poet makes us simultaneously aware of the earlier impressions and the new way of looking at them. This adds to the immediacy of the poem.

4.5.4 *Systemic Linguistics and Other Schools of Linguistics*

The concepts of chain and choice are not new or exclusive to systemic linguistics. The syntagmatic and paradigmatic axes have long been recognized in linguistics and are accepted by most schools of linguists.

However since the systemic model of language as a whole is different from other models it gives a different perspective to these concepts.

The systemic school of linguistics, perhaps more than any other school, stresses the importance of the notion of choice in relation to the paradigmatic axis. In fact it could be said that, to systemic linguists, choice is the most important of all of the various aspects of language. This is the main aim of systemic linguistics, to account for the choices of language. To discover, that is, the options that are available in the language of a particular community, and to account for the choice of one option rather than another in a particular situation. (Or, to use the terms that were used in Chapter 2, to discover the 'can do' and to account for the 'does' (2.1.2).)

5
Grammar: Structure

Chapters 3 and 4 have introduced the most basic concepts of the systemic model of language.

Within the main model of language as described so far, each level of language has its own model. This book will consider in turn the models of the different levels. The remainder of this volume will be devoted to the model of the level of grammar, the models of the other levels being discussed in Volume II.

The models of the different levels have certain features in common. Each model has a category which caters for its level's patterns along the axis of chain. Each model has a category which caters for the contrasting choices which its level allows. The present chapter introduces the category of the grammatical model which caters for its level's patterns along the axis of chain.

5.1 STRUCTURES: THEIR PLACES AND ELEMENTS

At the level of grammar, the patterns along the axis of chain are called *structures*.

Structures, in common with all other patterns, involve likeness and repetition. The sentences

Ex. 5.1 *Theodore opened the door politely*
Ex. 5.2 *Some people sing operatic arias in their bath*

are alike. Something observable in the first sentence recurs in the second. Because they are alike, because something from the first sentence is repeated in the second, we can say that they have the same pattern. This same pattern is found also in the sentences

Ex. 5.3 *The cat scratched Aunt Jemima by accident*
Ex. 5.4 *These mistakes were very common last year.*

The sentences Ex. 5.1–4 are alike in three main ways. Firstly, they are alike in that each can be divided into four parts.

Theodore	*opened*	*the door*	*politely*
Some people	*sing*	*operatic arias*	*in their bath*
The cat	*scratched*	*Aunt Jemima*	*by accident*
These mistakes	*were*	*very common*	*last year*

Because they can be divided into four parts we say that they have a structure which consists of four *places*.

Secondly, they are alike in the things which fill these places in structure; that is, in the *elements* of their structure. *Theodore, some people, the cat* and *these mistakes* are alike in that each is playing the same part in its respective sentence. Each is acting as the *subject* of its sentence. Similarly *opened, sing, scratched* and *were* are alike in that each is acting as the *predicator* of its sentence. *The door, operatic arias, Aunt Jemima* and *very common* are alike in that each is acting as the *complement* of its sentence. *Politely, in their bath, by accident, last year* are alike in that each is acting as the *adjunct* of its sentence. The four sentences Ex. 5.1–4 are alike in that the structure of each consists of the elements: subject, predicator, complement and adjunct.

SUBJECT	PREDICATOR	COMPLEMENT	ADJUNCT
Theodore	*opened*	*the door*	*politely*
Some people	*sing*	*operatic arias*	*in their bath*
The cat	*scratched*	*Aunt Jemima*	*by accident*
These mistakes	*were*	*very common*	*last year*

It may be useful at this point to include some helpful but unscientific definitions, in case the examples alone are not sufficient to enable readers to recognize subjects, predicators, complements and adjuncts.[1]

---

[1] The writer should perhaps make clear her views on definitions. In an introductory book definitions can be dangerous; sometimes they mislead more than they instruct. Definitions which attempt to be simple and incisive often leave loop-holes, so that some of the things which the definition should exclude are allowed to creep in, and so that some of the things which really belong are excluded. Definitions which endeavour to leave no loop-holes often become so general or so complex as to be quite valueless for the purpose of enabling someone to recognize the thing which is defined. Sometimes such definitions consist of terms which themselves need to be defined before the original definitions can be understood. Definitions, then, tend to be either helpful and inaccurate, or accurate and unhelpful. Wherever possible in this book, concepts have been explained by means of examples rather than by means of definitions. No one defines red or green for a young child. The child is shown red things and green things and told 'This is red', 'That is green'. The child learns to recognize red and green by being shown examples of them. It is possible to teach a large number of linguistic concepts by the same method. However it is sometimes necessary to use definitions to reinforce the examples and, when this is so, it is important to be clear which kind of definition is being used. In this book the writer has drawn attention to the definitions which are of the helpful but inaccurate kind.

The definitions in close type in this chapter, such as those on page 64, are all of the helpful but inaccurate kind.

A predicator is the verb part of a sentence.

A subject is the part of a sentence which answers the question 'Who or what?' in front of the verb.

'Who or what *opened the door politely*?'   '*Theodore.*'
'Who or what *sing operatic arias in their bath*?'   '*Some people.*'
'Who or what *scratched Aunt Jemima by accident*?'   '*The cat.*'
'Who or what *were very common last year*?'   '*These mistakes.*'

A complement is the part of a sentence which answers the question 'Who or what?' (or, if one wishes to be pedantic, 'Whom or what?') *after* the verb.

'*Theodore opened* who or what *politely*?'   '*The door.*'
'*Some people sing* who or what *in their bath*?'   '*Operatic arias.*'
'*The cat scratched* who or what *by accident*?'   '*Aunt Jemima.*'
'*These mistakes were* who or what *last year*?'   '*Very common.*'

An adjunct is the part of a sentence which answers any question other than 'Who or what?' after the verb.

'*Theodore opened the door* how?'   '*Politely.*'
'*Some people sing operatic arias* where?'   '*In their bath.*'
'*The cat scratched Aunt Jemima* why?'   '*By accident.*'
'*These mistakes were very common* when?'   '*Last year.*'

Readers familiar with traditional grammars will have realized that, in its handling of this kind of structure, systemic grammar does not differ very much from earlier grammars. The main difference is the inclusion of the traditional 'object' under the heading of *complement*. Systemic grammar does, in fact, recognize the distinction between the traditional object and the traditional complement, but does not consider it sufficiently clear-cut to be introduced in the initial stages of an analysis.

The third way in which sentences Ex. 5.1–4 are alike is that the structure of each contains only one *occurrence* of each of its elements. We can compare these sentences with the sentences

Ex. 5.5   *Some people sing loudly in their bath*
Ex. 5.6   *The cat made Aunt Jemima very angry.*

Like the previous four sentences, these sentences each have a structure consisting of four places. Unlike the first four sentences, however, sentence Ex. 5.5 has two occurrences of the element adjunct, *loudly* and *in their bath*, and no occurrence of the element complement. Ex. 5.6 has two occurrences of the element complement, *Aunt Jemima* and *very angry*, and no occurrence of the element adjunct.

Structures consist of places which are filled by occurrences of elements. By saying this we can account for three different kinds of likeness between different sentences.

The subject, predicator, complement and adjunct kind of structure is one kind of English grammatical structure. Another kind of English grammatical structure is exemplified by the underlined stretches of the sentences

Ex. 5.7 *The boys nextdoor are friends of my niece*

Ex. 5.8 *Old houses nearby were destroyed by the fire*

Ex. 5.9 *The mistakes were very common indeed*

Ex. 5.10 *John couldn't swim quite quickly enough.*

Each underlined stretch can be divided into three parts; each has a structure consisting of three places. In each underlined stretch the places are filled by the elements *modifier, headword* and *qualifier*.

Each underlined stretch has only one occurrence of each of these elements.

MODIFIER	HEADWORD	QUALIFIER
the	*boys*	*nextdoor*
old	*houses*	*nearby*
very	*common*	*indeed*
quite	*quickly*	*enough*

The underlined stretch of language in

Ex. 5.11 *Some old houses nearby were destroyed by the fire*

has a structure of four places, these places being filled by two occurrences of the element modifier and one occurrence of each of the elements headword and qualifier.

The underlined stretch of language in

Ex. 5.12 *Houses nearby were destroyed by the fire*

has a structure of two places, these places being filled by one occurrence of each of the elements headword and qualifier, there being no occurrence of the element modifier.

Again, unscientific definitions may be useful.
A headword is an essential word in a stretch of language.
We could say *Houses were destroyed by the fire* but we could not say *Old were destroyed by the fire* or *Nearby were destroyed by the fire*. We could say *The mistakes were common* but we could not say

The mistakes were very or *The mistakes were indeed.* We could say *Boys are friends of my niece* and *John couldn't swim quickly* but we could not say *The are friends of my niece* or *John couldn't swim quite.* We could say *Nextdoor are friends of my niece* but the utterance would no longer be recognizably the same utterance; the utterance as a whole would now have the structure adjunct, predicator, subject, instead of the structure subject, predicator, complement which is found in the original version of the utterance given in Ex. 5.7. We could say *John couldn't swim enough* but again the utterance would no longer be recognizably the same utterance as the original version in Ex. 5.10; we should have changed its meaning. This definition based on essentialness can be helpful but like all definitions it has its drawbacks.

Having picked out the headword in a stretch of language, we can then say that a modifier is any word which modifies, qualifies, describes or identifies the headword and which comes before the headword, while a qualifier is any word which modifies, qualifies, describes or identifies the headword and which comes *after* the headword.

Another kind of English grammatical structure is exemplified by the underlined stretches of the sentences

Ex. 5.13 *Peter swam just beyond John*

Ex. 5.14 *He got nearly to France*

Ex. 5.15 *The cat jumped right over it*

Ex. 5.16 *Soon after that Theodore said farewell.*

Each underlined stretch can be divided into three parts; each has a structure consisting of three places. In each underlined stretch the places are filled by the elements *before-preposition*, *preposition* and *completive*. Each underlined stretch has only one occurrence of each of these elements.

BEFORE-PREPOSITION	PREPOSITION	COMPLETIVE
just	*beyond*	*John*
nearly	*to*	*France*
right	*over*	*it*
soon	*after*	*that*

The term *preposition* is used here in the same way as it is used in traditional grammars.

A preposition used without anything following it gives one a sense of incompleteness. *He got nearly to* leaves one asking 'He got nearly to what?' A completive is a bit of language which completes a preposition.

A before-preposition is something which comes before a preposition and which modifies the preposition.

The preposition and the completive are both essential elements in this kind of structure.

A fourth kind of English grammatical structure is exemplified by the underlined stretches of the sentences

Ex. 5.17   *Theodore's Jaguar has run down a cat*

Ex. 5.18   *The books we were expecting have turned up at last*

Ex. 5.19   *Bill had rung up Mary every night that week*

Ex. 5.20   *The assistant secretary has taken over the secretaryship.*

Again the structure of each of these stretches of language has three places and again the places are filled by one occurrence of each of these elements. The elements of this kind of structure are *auxiliary verb*, *verb* and *extension of verb*.

AUXILIARY VERB	VERB	EXTENSION OF VERB
has	*run*	*down*
have	*turned*	*up*
had	*rung*	*up*
has	*taken*	*over*

The underlined stretch of the sentence

Ex. 5.21   *I could have been being examined by this time*

has four occurrences of the element auxiliary verb, one occurrence of the element verb, no occurrence of the element extension of verb.

The term *auxiliary verb* is used here as in traditional grammars.

The element verb is what is sometimes called a *full verb* in traditional grammars. It is the most important lexical item in the verb part of a sentence.

An extension of verb is an adverb which changes the meaning of the verb to which it is attached. *Run down* has a different meaning from *run*. *Turned up* has a different meaning from *turned*. *Rung up* has a different meaning from *rung*. *Taken over* has a different meaning from *taken*.

Readers are warned against too readily assigning the description *extension of verb* to a linguistic item. It is true that in

Ex. 5.22   *Theodore ran down a cat*

down is acting as the element extension of verb. But in

Ex. 5.23   *A spider ran down Theodore*

down is a preposition going with the completive *Theodore. Ran down* in Ex. 5.22 has a different meaning from the ordinary verb *ran* in Ex. 5.23. Verbs without extensions are probably more common in English than verbs with extensions.

A fifth kind of English grammatical structure is exemplified by the underlined stretches of language in the sentences

Ex. 5.24 *Debunkers of hypocrisy are not always popular*

Ex. 5.25 *Unkindnesses are sometimes unavoidable*

Ex. 5.26 *Paintings are always being stolen lately*

Ex. 5.27 *I can never find any paintpots when I want them*

Ex. 5.28 *He's not very good at saying boo to geese*

Ex. 5.29 *The warden did not approve of their goings-on*

Ex. 5.30 *Theodore was always very courteous to his sisters-in-law.*

Debunkers and *unkindnesses* each have a structure consisting of four places. The first place in each is filled by the element *prefix*, the second place by the element *base*, the third by the element *suffix*, and the fourth by the element *ending*. *Paintings* has a structure of three places filled by the elements base, suffix, ending. *Paintpots* has two occurrences of the base element and one occurrence of the element ending.

Geese has a base element which we find also in *goose*. It also has a change of vowel indicating plurality. We could perhaps describe this change of vowel as an *infix*.

Goings-on has a base, a suffix and an ending and then something else tacked on. We could perhaps call this something else an *addition*.

Sisters-in-law would then have the structure: base, ending, addition.

PREFIX	BASE	INFIX	SUFFIX	ENDING	ADDITION
de	*bunk*		*er*	*s*	
un	*kind*		*ness*	*es*	
	paint		*ing*	*s*	
	paint, pot			*s*	
	goose	*ee*			
	go		*ing*	*s*	*-on*
	sister			*s*	*-in-law*

The term *prefix* is used here as in traditional grammars. The base is the essential element in the structure, the one without which the others cannot occur. It is independent (*free*) while the others are dependent (*bound*). *Bunk, kind, paint, pot* can each occur on their own. *De, un, er, ness, ing, s* cannot occur without such items as *bunk, kind, paint, pot.*

A suffix is sometimes called a derivational ending. By means of such an ending one kind of word is derived from another kind of word. By means of the suffix *er*, the noun *painter* is derived from the verb *paint.* By means of the suffix *ness*, the noun *kindness* is derived from the adjective *kind.*

An ending specifies such information as number, person or tense. All the endings in the above examples indicate plurality. The *s* ending on the verb *knits* indicates singular, third person, present tense.

An infix has the same kind of function as an ending but takes the form of an internal modification to the base instead of something added on at the end. The change of vowel from *goose* to *geese* indicates plurality. The change of vowel from *ring* to *rang* indicates past tense.

An addition is something added on at the end even after the ending which is usually the last element in this kind of structure.

A sixth kind of English grammatical structure is exemplified by the sentences

Ex. 5.31 *After she had been scratched by the cat, Aunt Jemima shooed it away*

Ex. 5.32 *Since time is pressing, we'd better go*

Ex. 5.33 *If you like, I'll call for you.*

Each of these sentences has a structure of two places, the first being filled by a *subordinate* element of structure and the second being filled by a *main* element of structure.

SUBORDINATE	MAIN
After she had been scratched by the cat	*Aunt Jemima shooed it away*
Since time is pressing	*we'd better go*
If you like	*I'll call for you*

The structure of each of the sentences

Ex. 5.34 *I'll have my supper when you've finished*

Ex. 5.35 *Peter crossed the road because the pillar box was on the other side*

Ex. 5.36 *The cat, who was called Tiddles, scratched Aunt Jemima*

also consists of a subordinate element and a main element, but the two elements are now in a different order. In Ex. 5.34 and 5.35 the main element is followed by the subordinate element. In Ex. 5.36 the subordinate element occurs in the middle of the main element.

MAIN	SUBORDINATE
I'll have my supper	*when you've finished*
Peter crossed the road	*because the pillar box was on the other side*
The cat . . . scratched Aunt Jemima	*who was called Tiddles*

The structure of the sentence

Ex. 5.37 *He worked hard and he worked long hours, since time was so pressing*

has two occurrences of the main element and one occurrence of the subordinate element.

The structure of the sentence

Ex. 5.38 *If you like and if Bill doesn't mind, I'll call for you*

has two occurrences of the subordinate element and one occurrence of the main element.

The terms *main* and *subordinate* are used as in traditional grammars. The main element is the essential element of the structure, the independent (free) element. The subordinate element is the dependent (bound) element.

(Symbols or abbreviations are usually used for the elements of structure:

α = main element, β = subordinate element;
s = subject, p = predicator, c = complement, A = adjunct;
m = modifier, h = headword, q = qualifier;
b = before-preposition, p = preposition, c = completive;
a = auxiliary verb, v = verb, e = extension of verb.

Prefix, base, infix, suffix, ending and addition are written out in full.

An inventory of elements forming a structure is written with commas between the symbols. A particular structure, a particular combination of elements, is written without commas. Thus we say that the sentences

Ex. 5.39 *Yesterday the cat made Aunt Jemima very angry*
Ex. 5.40 *Yesterday, by accident, the cat scratched Aunt Jemima*

each have a structure composed of the elements s, p, c, A.
Ex. 5.39 has the structure ASPCC. Ex. 5.40 has the structure AASPC.

The stretches of language

Ex. 5.41   *The houses nearby*
Ex. 5.42   *The ten old thatched cottages nearby*

each have a structure composed of the elements *m, h, q*. Ex. 5.41 has the structure *mhq*. Ex. 5.42 has the structure *mmmmhq*.

When an element occurs in the middle of another element, we indicate this by placing the interrupting element in round brackets. Thus we say that

Ex. 5.43   *I have already told you*

has the structure SP(A)C. Similarly

Ex. 5.36   *The cat, who was called Tiddles, scratched Aunt Jemima*

has the structure α(β).)

5.2   STRUCTURES ARE 'COMPOUND' PATTERNS FORMED BY THE INTERACTION OF 'SIMPLE' PATTERNS

So far, all that this chapter has really done is to introduce a number of English grammatical structures and to discuss them in terms of their places and occurrences of elements. Very little attempt has yet been made to explain what such structures really are. It has been said that structures are grammatical patterns along the axis of chain and this is perfectly true as far as it goes, but further explanation is necessary.

We must distinguish between different kinds of pattern. We could perhaps distinguish between what we might call 'simple' patterns and what we might call 'compound' patterns. The word *compound* is being used here in a sense akin to its chemical sense—a complex substance forged by the combination of two or more simpler substances—rather than in its more usual grammatical sense. A 'compound' pattern is a pattern formed by the interaction of two or more 'simple' patterns.

> The words *simple* and *compound* are placed in inverted commas throughout this chapter to indicate that they are by no means technical terms of the theory. They are used merely to further the chemical analogy.

All the structures introduced in Section 5.1 are 'compound' patterns. Each structure is the result of the interaction of a number of 'simple' patterns.

Sections 5.2.1, 5.2.2, 5.2.3, 5.2.4 and 5.2.5 will consider some of the 'simple' patterns.

Section 5.2.6 will draw together the threads of what has been said about the 'simple' patterns and about the way in which they interact to form the 'compound' patterns.

5.2.1   Formal Items

The first kind of 'simple' pattern to be considered is the kind which consists of *formal items* occurring in sequences. This subsection will introduce the concept of the formal item and the following subsection will introduce the concept of sequence.

Formal items are actual bits of language which represent elements of structure.

The sentences

Ex. 5.1   *Theodore opened the door politely*
Ex. 5.2   *Some people sing operatic arias in their bath*
Ex. 5.3   *The cat scratched Aunt Jemima by accident*
Ex. 5.4   *These mistakes were very common last year*

each have an s element. In Ex. 5.1 the element s is represented by the formal item *Theodore*; in Ex. 5.2 it is represented by the formal item *some people*; in Ex. 5.3 by the formal item *the cat*; and in Ex. 5.4 by the formal item *these mistakes*.

Similarly these four sentences each have a P element. In Ex. 5.1 the element P is represented by the formal item *opened*; in Ex. 5.2 it is represented by the formal item *sing*; in Ex. 5.3 by the formal item *scratched*; and in Ex. 5.4 by the formal item *were*.

Any language will have a very large number of formal items, so large a number as to be uncountable. The language will, comparatively speaking, have a very small number of elements of grammatical structure.

This means that each element of structure can be represented by any one of a large number of formal items. An element of structure is more general, more abstract, than the formal items which represent it.

The formal items being discussed here are grammatical formal items. In many cases grammatical formal items are the same items as the lexical items, the formal items of lexis (see Chapter 3). *Theodore* in Ex. 5.1 is a grammatical formal item representing the element s. It is also a lexical item important in its own right as an individual item. For the moment readers may find it simpler to assume that grammatical formal items are the same thing as lexical items, though they are not quite the same thing, as will be explained in Volume II Chapter 3.

5.2.2 *Sequence*

The formal items which represent the elements of structure occur one after another in a *sequence*.

The position which a formal item occupies in a sequence is one of the clues which enable us to recognize the element of structure which the formal item is representing. In

Ex. 5.44   *John congratulated Theodore*

the formal item *John* is representing the element s.

In

Ex. 5.45   *Theodore congratulated John*

the same formal item, *John*, is representing a different element, the element c. We recognize that the formal item is representing s in Ex. 5.44 but c in Ex. 5.45 partly from the fact that in Ex. 5.44 it occurs before *congratulated* whereas in Ex. 5.45 it occurs after *congratulated*.

However, the recognition of an element of structure from the position in sequence of the formal item which represents it is not such a straightforward matter as examples Ex. 5.44 and 5.45 make it appear, since the elements of a structure do not always occur in the same order.

For any structure it is possible to state the usual order of the elements. But unusual orders also occur.

The most usual order of elements for the s, p, c, a kind of structure, for example, is spca (though certain kinds of adjunct more usually occur in other positions). But psca, cpsa, aspc and various other combinations and permutations are also possible.

In order to recognize an element of structure from the position in sequence of a formal item it is necessary to take into account the unusual orders of elements of the structure as well as the most usual order.

The most usual order of elements for a structure is called the *unmarked* version of the structure. The unmarked version, because it is the most usual, is the one we expect. Because it is the one we expect, it is the one we notice least. There is nothing in it to mark it out in such a way as to particularly attract our attention.

The less usual orders of elements are *marked* versions of the structure. They run counter to our expectancy. Their unusualness attracts our attention and marks them out as being something different from the ordinary. This is why

Ex. 4.2 *Authority I respect but authoritarianism I deplore*

is, as suggested in Chapter 4, more emphatic than

Ex. 4.3 *I respect authority but I deplore authoritarianism.*

Each half of Ex. 4.2 has the structure CSP, a marked version of the S, P, C, A kind of structure. Each half of Ex. 4.3 has the structure SPC, the unmarked version of the structure. Ex. 4.2 attracts more attention than Ex. 4.3.

In this subsection then, we have been considering the first of our 'simple' kinds of pattern, that consisting of formal items occurring in certain sequences. We have also returned to a consideration of the 'compound' kind of pattern introduced in Section 5.1, that consisting of elements of structure occurring in certain orders. We have seen something of the relationship between the 'simple' kind of pattern and the 'compound' kind of pattern: sequences of formal items represent orders of elements. The sequences of formal items can provide us with clues to the elements of structure and their orders.

5.2.3 *Class*

The formal items which occur in sequences can be divided into *classes*. Any formal item is more likely to represent certain elements of structure than to represent others, and on this basis it can be assigned to a class.

The formal items *opened, sing, scratched, were, has run down, have turned up, had rung up, has taken over, couldn't swim* are all more likely to represent the element P than to represent any other element. On this basis we can group them together and, with all the other formal items like them, assign them to a particular class. The name which we give to this class of items, the class of items which usually represent the element P, is the *verbal group*.

Similarly the formal items *politely, in their bath, by accident, last year, just beyond John, nearly to France, right over it, soon after that* are all more likely to represent the element A than to represent any other element. These items too can be grouped together with all the other formal items like them and assigned to a particular class. This class of items is called the *adverbial group*.

The element P, then, has a class of items which usually represent it and so too does the element A. The items in P's class are unlikely to represent any other element of structure; P has its class of items all to itself, as it were. The element A's class of items is similarly reasonably distinct from other classes of item; most of its items are unlikely to represent any other element.

Sometimes however there is quite a lot of overlap between the items of one class and the items of another. Most, though not all, of the items in the class which represent the element S are equally likely to represent the element C and most, though not all, of the items in the class which represent the element C are equally likely to represent the element S.

Of the formal items which represent S and C in examples Ex. 5.1–4, *very common* is much more likely to represent C than S, but all the others —*Theodore, the door, some people, operatic arias, the cat, Aunt Jemima, these mistakes*—are just as likely to represent S as C and vice versa.

In a case such as this where there is such a great deal of overlap between two classes, we combine the two classes into a *cross-class*; that is, we fuse the two classes into one and treat them as if they were indeed one class.

The cross-class of items which represent S and/or C is called the *nominal group*.

The class of an item is, like sequence, one of the clues which enable us to recognize the element of structure that the item is representing in a given stretch of language. In

Ex. 5.44   *John congratulated Theodore*
Ex. 5.45   *Theodore congratulated John*

we recognize that *congratulated* is representing the element P, partly from the fact that *congratulated* is a verbal group (i.e. a member of the verbal group class of items). We would still recognize it as the element P even if it did not occur in the expected position in sequence. In Thomas Hardy's lines

Ex. 5.46   *Perhaps Thy ancient rote-restricted ways*
            Thy ripening rule transcends;

the fact that *transcends* is a verbal group enables us to recognize that it is representing the element P, even though the elements are here in an unusual order.

What is happening here is that the potential is being used as a clue to the actual. If an item belongs to a class of items which are potentially very likely to be representing a certain element, then it is fair to assume that in a given stretch of language the item will actually be representing that element unless there is any information to the contrary.

Like sequence, however, class is not an infallible clue to structure. We must again allow for unusual forms of language as well as for usual forms. We cannot assume that a particular formal item will always represent an element of structure which it is likely to represent or that it will never represent an element of structure which it is unlikely to represent.

E. E. Cummings provides an extreme example of discrepancy between class and structure in *anyone lived in a pretty how town*.

Ex. 5.47   *he sang his didn't he danced his did*

Both *didn't* and *did* belong to the class of item which usually represents the element *a* (auxiliary verb), but in this line each represents the element *h* (headword) in the structure *mh*.

5.2.4   *Type*

So far under the heading of 'simple' patterns we have been looking at a kind of pattern consisting of sequences of formal items which are members of classes.

Formal items are also members of *types*.

When we divide formal items into classes, we are dividing them on the basis of their likeness in potentiality for representing a certain element or elements of structure. When we divide formal items into types, we are dividing them on the basis of their own structure.

If we were to divide into classes the formal items *scratched, couldn't swim, has run down, have turned up, very politely, quite quickly enough, just beyond John, nearly to France, the door, operatic arias, the boys next door, old houses nearby* we should arrive at the following groupings, since the items in the first column are most likely to represent the element P, the items in the second column to represent the element A, the items in the third column to represent the element s or the element c.

VERBAL GROUPS	ADVERBIAL GROUPS	NOMINAL GROUPS
scratched	*very politely*	*the door*
couldn't swim	*quite quickly enough*	*operatic arias*
has run down	*just beyond John*	*the boys next door*
have turned up	*nearly to France*	*old houses nearby*

If we were to divide the same formal items into types on the basis of their own structure, we should arrive at rather different groupings. The items no longer necessarily occur in the same columns.

a, v, e TYPE	*b, p, c* TYPE	*m, h, q* TYPE
scratched	*just beyond John*	*very politely*
couldn't swim	*nearly to France*	*quite quickly enough*
has run down		*the door*
have turned up		*operatic arias*
		the boys nextdoor
		old houses nearby

As in the case of class, there is a potential/actual relationship between type of item and element of structure. Just as we can use the class of an item as a clue to the element of structure represented by the item, so too can we use the type of the item.

The relationship between type of item and element of structure is actually more complex than the relationship between class of item and element of structure. The relationship between class and type is more complex still. A full discussion of these relationships is beyond the scope of this book, though some indications of the complexities will be given in Chapter 7.

5.2.5. *Function*

In the previous four subsections we have been considering 'simple' patterns consisting of sequences of formal items which are members of classes and sequences of formal items which are members of types. We now come to a very different kind of 'simple' pattern.

Each element of structure has certain *functions* associated with it.

The element s, for instance, usually has the function of expressing the *actor* of an action. It also usually has the function of expressing the *theme* of a sentence; that is, it refers to the topic about which the rest of the sentence is a comment. The element s also acts as a *mood marker*; that is, it is the stretch of a language which, by its position relative to the predicator, indicates whether a sentence is a statement or a question. A fourth function which s usually has is that of *number and person marker*; that is, it is the stretch of language which is related to the predicator in such a way as to determine the number and person of the predicator.

In the example

Ex. 5.48   *John has gone to work by bus each day this week*

the element s is represented by the formal item *John*. 'John' is the actor
of the action of going. 'John' is also the theme of the sentence, the
topic about which the rest of the sentence is providing information.
'John' is also a mood marker; the fact that *John* comes before *has gone*
instead of in the middle of it indicates that the sentence is a statement,
not a question. 'John' is also a number and person marker; it deter-
mines that the form of the predicator will be *has gone* rather than *have
gone*.

Function is yet another of the clues which enable us to recognize the
element of structure that an item is representing in a given stretch of
language.

We recognize that in example Ex. 5.48 the formal item *John* is
representing the element s partly because of its position in sequence,
partly because it is a nominal group (though this could equally well
suggest that it is representing the element c), partly because of its type,
partly because it has the functions which we normally associate with the
element s.

However, function is no more infallible as a clue than sequence and
class. We can say with confidence that in example Ex. 5.48 the formal
item *John* is representing the element s, since it has all four of the
functions usually associated with the element s. Indeed in unmarked
(usual) forms of language these four functions always do go together
and always are associated with the element s. In marked (unusual)
forms of language, however, the functions are often separated and
distributed over different stretches of language in order that different
shades of emphasis may be conveyed. In

Ex. 5.49   *John was given a lift to work by Mr Jackson*

John is still performing the functions of theme, mood marker and
number and person marker, but it is no longer expressing the actor of
an action. 'Mr Jackson' is the actor of the action of giving.

In the example from Chapter 4

Ex. 4.2   *Authority I respect but authoritarianism I deplore*

I is in each half performing the functions of actor, mood marker and
number and person marker. But 'authority' is what the first half of the
sentence is really about and 'authoritarianism' is what the second half
of the sentence is really about. *Authority* is performing the function of

theme in the first half of the sentence, while *authoritarianism* is performing the function of theme in the second half of the sentence.

Mood marker and number and person marker are the two functions which most regularly go together. But even these two can be split in certain kinds of construction. In

Ex. 5.50   *There are six books on that table*

there is performing the function of mood marker; if we wanted to turn the statement into a question, we should have to change the position of *there* in relation to the predicator and say *Are there six books on that table?* But *six books* is performing the function of number and person marker; if we were to change *six books* to *a book*, we should have to change the form of the predicator from *are* to *is*.

So far in this subsection we have been considering functions associated with the element s. The other elements also have functions associated with them.

The functions associated with elements of structure, themselves form patterns.

For instance the sentences

Ex. 5.3   *The cat scratched Aunt Jemima by accident*
Ex. 5.51   *John kicked the door in a temper*

each have the functional pattern actor + *action* + *goal* (the person or thing at which the action is directed) + *circumstance*.

ACTOR	ACTION	GOAL	CIRCUMSTANCE
The cat	*scratched*	*Aunt Jemima*	*by accident*
John	*kicked*	*the door*	*in a temper*

The two sentences also each have the functional pattern theme + *rheme* (the comment which is made about the theme of the sentence).

THEME	RHEME
The cat	*scratched Aunt Jemima by accident*
John	*kicked the door in a temper*

A third functional pattern which the two sentences have is that of *mood marker*[1] + *mood marker*[2] + *support* (the rest of the message).

MOOD MARKER[1]	MOOD MARKER[2]	SUPPORT
The cat	*scratched*	*Aunt Jemima by accident*
John	*kicked*	*the door in a temper*

A fourth functional pattern which the two sentences have is very similar to the third, consisting of *number and person marker*[1] + *number and person marker*[2] + *remainder*.

Any sentence will, like the two sentences discussed here, have layers of functional patterns superimposed on each other.

5.2.6 *The Interaction of the 'Simple' Patterns*

Section 5.1, the section which introduced the 'compound' patterns, began by drawing attention to the likenesses between Ex. 5.1, 5.2, 5.3 and 5.4. The first likeness to which it drew attention was that each sentence could be divided into four parts. No explanation was given, however, of why it was possible to divide the sentences into four parts. Such an explanation can now be given.

Let us take just one of the four sentences by way of example and consider it in relation to the 'simple' patterns which have just been discussed.

FIGURE 5.1

Ex. 5.3	*The cat*	*scratched*	*Aunt Jemima*	*by accident*
Class of formal item	nominal group	verbal group	nominal group	adverbial group
Type of formal item	*m, h, q*	*a, v, e*	*m, h, q*	*p, c*
Functional patterns	actor	action	goal	circumstance
	mood marker[1]	mood marker[2]	support	
	number and person marker[1]	number and person marker[2]	remainder	
	theme	rheme		

It can be seen from the analysis in Figure 5.1 that all the 'simple' patterns discussed in this chapter combine to suggest that, if we are going to split Ex. 5.3 into its component parts, we should make a cut between *the cat* and *scratched*. Most of the 'simple' patterns combine to suggest a cut between *scratched* and *Aunt Jemima*. A number of the 'simple' patterns suggest a cut between *Aunt Jemima* and *by accident*.

Our division into four parts of the structure, the 'compound' pattern, of this sentence is then the result of the combined force of the 'simple' patterns.

Just as a structure as a whole is the result of the interaction of these 'simple' patterns, so too are the individual elements. The s element of Ex. 5.3, for instance, is an s element because the formal item representing it, *the cat*, is occurring at the beginning of the sentence, because the formal item is a member of the nominal group class of items, because the formal item is of the *m, h, q* type of item, and because it has the functions of actor, theme, mood marker[1] and number and person marker[1].

In Ex. 5.3 the 'simple' patterns are all in step, as it were. They all lead us to very much the same conclusion about the 'compound' pattern of the sentence. This is not the case with all sentences, however.

In most of the subsections of Section 5.2 some attention has been paid to marked (less usual) forms of language. A marked form of language is one in which one (or more) of the 'simple' patterns is out of step with the other 'simple' patterns. In

Ex. 5.49   *John was given a lift to work by Mr Jackson*

the actor + action + goal + circumstance functional pattern is out of step since the actor is no longer, as it usually is, aligned with the theme, mood marker[1] and number and person marker[1].

In both halves of

Ex. 4.2   *Authority I respect but authoritarianism I deplore*

the theme + rheme pattern is out of step since the theme is no longer aligned with its usual associates, the actor, mood marker[1] and number and person marker.[1]

It is the clash between the 'simple' patterns which gives these marked forms of language their attention-drawing quality.

We can still assign a structure to such sentences but the structure will be less clear-cut and more controversial than in the case of unmarked forms of language.

For instance when trying to locate the s element in a marked form of language we have to decide whether to follow the evidence of the majority of 'simple' patterns and assign the label s to the stretch of language which has the largest number of the characteristics associated with the element s, or whether to single out a particular 'simple' pattern as being somehow more fundamental than the others and to assign the label s on the basis of the part played by a stretch of language in that particular 'simple' pattern. In fact the latter course is usually followed. The mood marker[1] + mood marker[2] + support pattern is usually singled out as the most fundamental, and the label s is assigned to the stretch of language which has the function mood marker[1]. Separate statements are then made in order to map the other 'simple' patterns on to the most fundamental 'simple' pattern. (See Volume II, Chapter 2.)

At the beginning of the chapter, structures were introduced simply as patterns. We can now go a step further and say that structures are patterns which are the result of the interaction of a number of other patterns.

Two points should be made here in order to counteract any distorted impressions which readers have received from this chapter.

Firstly, in this chapter patterns consisting of sequences of formal items have been lumped together with patterns consisting of sets of functions, under the heading of 'simple' patterns. In fact patterns consisting of sequences of formal items are very different from patterns consisting of sets of functions. The relationship between structures and patterns consisting of sequences of formal items is very different from the relationship between structures and patterns consisting of sets of functions. These differences will be shown in Volume II Chapter 2.

Secondly, the 'simple' patterns discussed in this chapter are by no means an exhaustive list of the patterns which interact to form structures. The patterns discussed in relation to Ex. 5.3 are by no means the only patterns which are relevant to the s, p, c, a kind of structure. And there are yet more patterns which are relevant to other structures. There is a similar set of patterns, for instance, which lead us to ascribe the structure *mhq* to *the boys next door*; and another set which lead us to ascribe the structure *bpc* to *just beyond John*.

5.3 DEPTH

At the beginning of this chapter each exemplifying sentence was discussed in relation to only one kind of structure. However if we are to fully describe the structure of a stretch of language, we need to consider it in relation to a number of kinds of structure, in fact to all the kinds of structure found in the language to which it belongs.

For example, the sentence

Ex. 5.52 *When the bus broke down, the boys walked to school*

has the structure βα. The β part of it has the structure ASP. The α part has the structure SPA. The separate parts of the ASP structure have, respectively, the structures *h*, *mh*, *ve*. The separate parts of the SPA structure have, respectively, the structures *mh*, *v*, *pc*. Each of the words in the sentence has the structure base, except for *boys* and *walked* which

have the structure base + ending, and *broke* which has the structure
base + infix (see Figure 5.2).

FIGURE 5.2   *The Structures of Ex. 5.52*

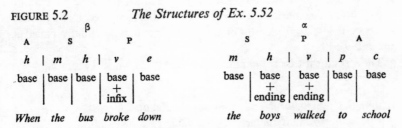

What we have done to Ex. 5.52 in the previous paragraph is to make a
series of cuts in it. The first cut split it into two parts. The next set of
cuts split each of these two parts into three parts. The next set of cuts
split each of the resulting six parts into parts. And so on, until we reached
a set of parts which could not meaningfully be split into any smaller
parts. (As we saw in Section 5.2, our reason for making each set of
cuts lies in the interaction of a number of 'simple' patterns.)

Different structures appeared at different stages of the cutting process.
We can in fact arrange the structures of a given stretch of language on
a scale according to the stages of the cutting process at which they
appeared, the structures which appeared earliest in the cutting process
coming at the top of the scale, the structures which appeared latest
coming at the bottom. We call this scale the scale of *depth*.

This kind of analysis, in which we make a series of sets of cuts in a
stretch of language in order to arrive at its structures, is sometimes
called *immediate constituent (IC)* analysis.

The order of the cuts we make in a sentence depends on the immediacy of the constituents. Initially one cut was made in Ex. 5.52 splitting it into two parts, since these two parts—*When the bus broke
down* and *the boys walked to school*—were considered to be the
immediate constituents of the sentence. *When*, *the bus* and *broke
down* are constituents of the sentence, but they are not the immediate
constituents since they can be combined to form another constituent, *When the bus broke down*. *When*, *the bus* and *broke down* are
immediate constituents of *When the bus broke down*; they are the
immediate constituents of an immediate constituent of the sentence
as a whole. *The* and *bus* are constituents of *When the bus broke down*,
but they are not immediate constituents since they can be combined
to form another constituent *the bus*.

The scale of depth arranges the structures of a stretch of language
according to whether their elements are immediate constituents of the
stretch of language, ultimate constituents of the stretch of language,
or something in between.

We usually represent the scale of depth for a stretch of language pictorially in a *tree-diagram*. (The use of tree-diagrams, sometimes jokingly referred to as 'arborization', is fashionable in linguistics as in a number of other disciplines!) The kind of tree-diagram used in linguistics to show the relative depths of different structures is usually called a *structural tree*.

The structural tree for example Ex. 5.52 is shown in Figure 5.3.

FIGURE 5.3   *Structural Tree Showing the Relative Depths
of the Structures of Ex. 5.52*

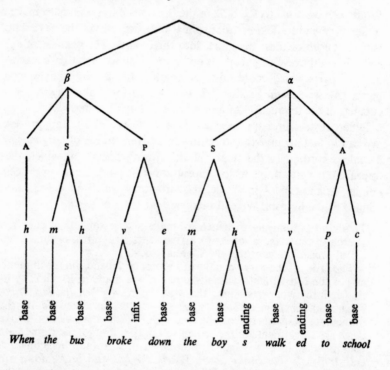

A structural tree has *layers*, the lines of symbols representing elements of structure, and *nodes*, the points at which branching takes place or at which branching might have taken place. (It is because it shows relationships by means of branching lines that a tree-diagram is called a 'tree' diagram.)

In Figure 5.4 the structural tree of Ex. 5.52 is shown with its layers and nodes labelled.

FIGURE 5.4   *Structural Tree of Ex. 5.52 Showing Layers and Nodes*

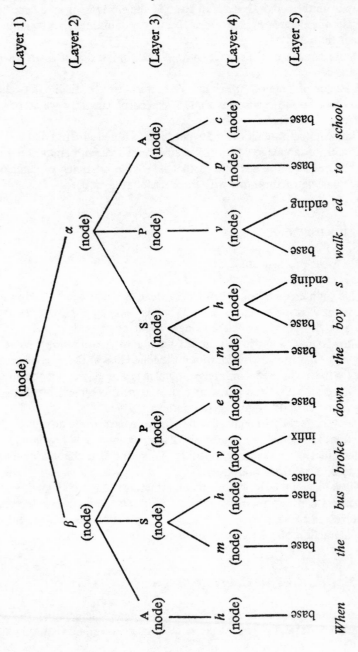

The depth of an element of structure is the number of nodes it is away from the top of the tree. In Ex. 5.52 the element α is at a depth of one and the element p (preposition) is at a depth of three; p is two nodes deeper than α.

Depth can be used as a measure of the complexity of a stretch of language.

A stretch of language which has a structural tree consisting of twenty layers will be more complex than a stretch of language which has a structural tree consisting of ten layers.

Similarly the number of nodes per layer is a measure of complexity. A stretch of language which has a structural tree with eight nodes at layer 3 will be more complex at that layer than a stretch of language which has a structural tree with three nodes at layer 3.

5.4 DISCUSSION

5.4.1 *General Linguistics*

In this chapter, as in the previous chapters, we have been working towards answers to the questions: What is language? How does language work? What have all languages got in common?

This chapter's contribution to an answer to the question: What is language? has been an exploration of the idea that at the level of grammar (as indeed at the other levels) language is a patterned phenomenon. We have seen that the patterning is extremely complex, involving a large number of different kinds of pattern.

The very fact that language is patterned is part of the answer to the question: How does language work? Language must have regularity and pattern if it is to have any meaning. To speak of a chaotic language would be a contradiction in terms.

All languages have grammatical structures. In all languages the structures can be described in terms of number of places, elements, occurrences of elements. In all languages structures are the result of the interaction of a number of other patterns.

5.4.2 *Descriptive and Contrastive Linguistics*

When describing and contrasting two different languages, or two different historical phases of the same language, we find that although they both have structures they do not necessarily have exactly the same structures. We also find that although in both languages structures are recognized through awareness of a number of other patterns, the clues to structure vary in relative importance from language to language. Sequence, for instance, cannot be used as a clue in the description of Latin in quite the same way as it can be used in the description of English. Sequence cannot be used in quite the same way in the description of Old English as it can in the description of present-day English.

When contrasting two different registers we find that for the most part they have basically the same structures and the difference between the registers lies rather in the frequency with which particular structures are used.

For instance, we find that some registers use αα structures more frequently than αβ structures, while for other registers the opposite is true. We find that some registers make more use of modifiers while other registers make more use of qualifiers. We find that some registers make great use of auxiliary verbs, while other registers make very little use of them.

We also find that certain kinds of marked structure occur more frequently in some registers than in others. The marked structure exemplified in

Ex. 5.53 *It's very nice, that bacon*
Ex. 5.54 *It's a mountain to be respected, Snowdon*

in which the s element is repeated, though in a different form (*it* and *that bacon, it* and *Snowdon*), is much more frequently found in impromptu spoken English than in written English.

As has already been said, basically registers have the same structures and differ only in the frequency with which they use particular structures. However there are a few structures which are peculiar to certain registers.

Almost all kinds of structure have marked versions which contrast with their unmarked versions. But the marked versions of some structures are more unusual than the marked versions of others.

We have seen that the CSP structure is a marked structure, unusual in comparison with SPC, the unmarked version of the structure, and that as a result of its comparative unusualness it attracts attention. It must be realized, however, that the unusualness is relative. The CSP structure does, in fact, occur very frequently in English. It is only in comparison with the SPC structure, which occurs much more frequently, that the csp structure can be considered unusual. The csp structure is a quite usual kind of marked structure.

Marked versions of the *b*, *p*, *c* kind of structure, on the other hand, are very unusual. In most varieties of present-day English the *bpc* order is invariable. It is only in registers such as literary language and the language of advertising, in which writers specialize in linguistic innovation, that we find marked versions of the *b*, *p*, *c* kind of structure.

E. E. Cummings in

Ex. 5.55   *Me up at does*
                        out of the floor
                        quietly stare
                        a poisoned mouse

is not only using a marked version of the s, p, c, a kind of structure—AP(AA)s. In the first three words *Me up at* he is also using a marked version of the *b*, *p*, *c* kind of structure, the completive *Me* coming before its preposition instead of after it.

By using two different kinds of marked structure in the same stretch of language, E. E. Cummings immediately attracts attention.

There are also more precise reasons why his structures are ordered in this way. The poem is, among other things, about the relative positions of its protagonists, relative positions both in physical terms and in moral or ethical terms. It is fitting that the poet should draw attention to the relative physical and moral positions of his protagonists by the relative positions of his elements of structure.

In general it is true to say that the first half of the poem, the four lines quoted above, is mainly concerned with the relative physical positions of the protagonists while the second half of the poem is more concerned with the relative moral positions. However the poem is ordered in such a way that the moral issues of the second half of the poem are foreshadowed in the first half of the poem and in such a way that the perspectives of the first half of the poem are summarized in the first three words. Thus the three words which, by means of marked structures, have been placed at the beginning of the poem can be said to epitomize the first half of the poem which in turn epitomizes the poem as a whole.

The very first word *Me* makes us aware that the poem concerns two protagonists. Since the form *Me* is used instead of *I* we know that we are being introduced to the second of two protagonists rather than to the one and only protagonist. Thus *Me* actually refers to one protagonist and implies another. The next two words *up at* show us that the poem is concerned with the distance and perspective between the two protagonists. The first half of the poem as a whole makes explicit what is implied in the first three words. The protagonists are actually named: *Me* and *a poisoned mouse*. They are given prominence since each is in an emphatic position owing to the placing of the element which it represents. They are at opposite ends of the clause separated by a longish stretch of language which expresses the distance and perspective between them.

As has been said, just as the first three words *Me up at* imply all that is explicitly stated in the first half of the poem, the first half of the poem foreshadows what is later made more explicit in the poem as a whole. One of the things that contributes to this foreshadowing is the position of *Me*. *Me* has been thrust forward by the combined force of the two marked structures. This gives it something of the effect of the *Me* uttered by someone against whom an accusation has been made.

> For those who are not familiar with the poem it should perhaps be pointed out that the poem is multiply ambiguous. The remarks made above are inevitably an oversimplification of the poem and its structures. A full discussion of the poem would of course be out of place in a book of this kind.

5.4.3 Applied Linguistics

Grammatical structural analysis has many uses in applied linguistics. For instance it can be used in the description of children's language in order to show how children's speech and writing develop grammatically as the children grow older, or in order to show how children's language varies in relation to such factors as IQ or social background. Such studies are relevant to language teaching, to psycholinguistics and to sociolinguistics.

Various attempts have been made to show that children use more complex language as they grow older. The scale of depth could well be used as a measure of complexity in a study of this kind. (See Section 5.3.)

With regard to the application of grammatical structural analysis to literary studies, it can be said that it is relevant to ask about a literary work: Why has the writer used the grammatical structures that he has used? It is an interesting and often revealing exercise to rewrite a literary passage, deliberately using different structures from those of the original, and then to ask oneself what the passage has lost in the change. It is too often assumed that the meaning of a literary text is given to it by its lexical items. This is, of course, partly true, but it should always be remembered that the grammar too is meaningful. (More will be said about the meaningfulness of grammar later in this book, particularly in Chapters 8 and 9; and in Volume II Chapters 2 and 6.)

5.4.4 *Systemic Linguistics and Other Schools of Linguistics*

Systemic linguistics is like other schools of linguistics in recognizing that the grammar of a language has structures. Like other schools it describes stretches of language by splitting them up and applying labels which show how the parts relate to each other and how the parts relate to the whole.

It is also like most other modern schools in recognizing that there is a great deal more to grammar than can be indicated by a structural analysis of this kind. The following chapters of this book will show how systemic linguistics deals with the aspects of grammar which are not fully covered by a structural description.

> In some ways it could be said that by considering structures before systems we have begun at the wrong end of systemic grammar. The order of the presentation of the book was selected as a result of the wish to lead readers from the familiar to the unfamiliar. It was felt that structural descriptions of the kind presented in this chapter were more akin than later parts of the book to the kinds of grammatical analysis which readers would probably have met at school.

Systemic linguistics differs from other schools in that it regards a structure as a complex entity resulting from the interaction of a number of different patterns. It regards a structural description of the kind given in this chapter as a summary of the different patterns which have been perceived in a stretch of language.

Systemic linguistics also differs from other schools in the importance it attaches to the unmarked/marked distinction in language. This is due to its readiness to discuss language in terms of statistical probabilities rather than in terms of a clearcut acceptable/not acceptable distinction (2.1.4 and 2.1.5).

6
Grammar: Unit

6.1 UNITS

In Chapter 5 elements of structure were shown to be represented by formal items. These formal items are of different sizes. The different sizes of formal items are called *units*.

Units of grammar are much like the units of measurement. For linear measurements we work with such things as yards, feet and inches, or metres, centimetres and millimetres; in grammar we work with such things as sentences and words. In each case the smaller units combine to form the larger units; or, to look at it another way, the larger units consist of the smaller units.

In grammar each unit can be identified in two ways: by the way in which it combines with other units to form larger units and by the combination of smaller units of which it is itself composed. In other words it can be identified by the part it plays in the structure of a larger unit and also by its own structure.

The units of English grammar include the *sentence*, the *clause*, the *group*, the *word* and the *morpheme*. The unit at each end of this list is rather a special case, so I shall begin by discussing the middle three units.

Clauses, like other units, can be identified by the part they play in the structure of a larger unit and also by their own structure. Any clause will be playing the part of an α element or a β element in a sentence. It will have a structure which consists of one or more of the elements S, P, C, A. In

Ex. 6.1

β

A	S	P	A
When	Aunt Jemima	returned	from Basingstoke,

When Aunt Jemima returned from Basingstoke,

α

S	P	C	A
Theodore	met	her	at the station

Theodore met her at the station

there are two clauses. In

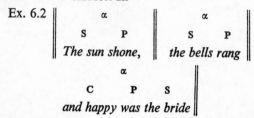

Ex. 6.2

α		α
S P		S P
The sun shone,		*the bells rang*

α
C   P   S
and happy was the bride

there are three clauses. (A pair of vertical lines is the usual way of marking the boundary of a clause.)

Systemic grammar differs slightly at this point from traditional grammar. Most traditional grammars would not consider as clauses the underlined sections of the following sentences:

Ex. 6.3   *Whistling merrily, he cycled down the road*
Ex. 6.4   *His job finished, he went home*
Ex. 6.5   *To win the prize, he must work harder.*

But each of the underlined sections is acting as a β element in a sentence, just as is each of the underlined sections of the following sentences:

Ex. 6.6   *John, who was whistling merrily, cycled down the road*
Ex. 6.7   *When his job was finished, he went home*
Ex. 6.8   *If he is to win the prize, he must work harder.*

Also, *Whistling merrily* has the structure PA, *His job finished* has the structure SP and *To win the prize* has the structure PC. So each has the kind of structure which is characteristic of a clause. For these reasons, systemic grammar considers *Whistling merrily, His job finished, To win the prize* and other stretches of language like them to be clauses.

Any group will be playing the part of an S element, a P element, a C element or an A element in the structure of a clause. It will have a structure which consists of one or more of the elements m, h, q or one or more of the elements b, p, c or one or more of the elements a, v, e. In

A	S	P		C	
h	h	a	v	m	h
Yesterday	*I*	*was visiting*		*my sister*	

Ex. 6.9

there are four groups. In

S			P	C	
m	m	h	v	m	h
Our nextdoor neighbour			*mended*	*the fuse*	

Ex. 6.10

there are three groups. (A single vertical line is the usual way of marking the boundary of a group.)

Any word will be playing the part of one of the elements *m*, *h*, *q*, *b*, *p*, *c*, *a*, *v*, *e* in the structure of a group. It will have a structure which consists of one or more of the elements base, prefix, infix, suffix, ending, addition. In

	m	*h*		*v*		*m*	*h*
	base	base	suffix ending	base	ending	base	base
Ex. 6.11	*The*	*painters*		*finished*		*the*	*room*

there are five words. (As in traditional orthography, the usual way of marking the boundary of a word is by leaving a space.)

Any morpheme will be playing the part of one of the elements base, prefix, infix, suffix, ending, addition, in the structure of a word. In

	base	suffix	ending
		+	+
Ex. 6.12	*paint*	*er*	*s*

there are three morphemes. In

	base	suffix	ending	addition
		+	+	+
Ex. 6.13	*go*	*ing*	*s*	*-on*

there are four morphemes. (The usual way of marking the boundary of a morpheme is by the sign + .)

A morpheme can be identified in one way only, by reference to the part it plays in the structure of a word. A morpheme has no grammatical structure of its own. 'Having structure' implies that something is made up of things smaller than itself. The morpheme is the smallest grammatical unit and therefore there are no smaller things from which it can be constructed.

A sentence, like a morpheme, can be identified in one way only. A sentence does have a structure of its own, but, being the largest grammatical unit, it cannot play a part in the structure of a larger unit.

A sentence's own structure will consist of one or more of the elements α, β, as in the following sentences:

Ex. 6.14 ‖ β *When night came,* ‖ α *he was far from home* ‖

Ex. 6.15 ‖ α *He huffed* ‖ α *and he puffed,* ‖ β *till he blew the house down* ‖

Ex. 6.16 ‖ α *The farmer drove the dog out of the field.* ‖

(Three vertical lines mark the boundary of a sentence.)

(Readers will have noticed that a different kind of lettering has been used for the structure of each unit mentioned so far. Greek letters symbolize the elements of sentence structure, capital letters the elements of clause structure, and lower case letters the elements of group structure, while the names of the elements of word structure have been written out in full.)

The sentence has been described above as the largest grammatical unit in English. It is possible that a case could be made out for a larger grammatical unit: the paragraph.

In the earlier chapters of this book the terms *sentence* and *word* were used rather loosely. For instance, the term *sentence* was sometimes used where the term *clause* would have been more appropriate. Now that the units have been introduced and defined, the terms referring to them will be used more precisely. Throughout the rest of the book it can be assumed that the terms *sentence, clause, group, word* and *morpheme* are used in the technical senses assigned to them in this chapter.

Units, then, are sizes of formal items. They are characterized by the elements of structure which they represent and/or by the structures which they themselves carry.

6.2 COMPLEX UNITS

In

Ex. 6.17 ‖ S
m m h | m m h
The men's halls | *and the women's halls*
P | A
are | *on different sides of the campus* ‖

The men's halls and the women's halls could be said to be a group. It certainly satisfies the first half of the definition of a group given earlier in the chapter, since it is acting as the s element of a clause. There is a sense in which it also satisfies the second half of the definition, since it has a structure which consists of one or more of the elements *m, h, q*. However, as far as the second half of the definition is concerned, there is also a sense in which *The men's halls and the women's halls* could be said to be more than one set of *m, h, q* elements. It is divisible into two parts each of which has the structure characteristic of a group. *The men's halls and the women's halls* is a *complex group*.

Similarly, in

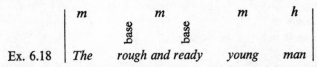

Ex. 6.18

rough and ready could be said to be a word. It satisfies the first half of the definition of a word given earlier, since it is acting as the *m* element of a group. It satisfies the second half of the definition, since it has a structure which consists of one or more of the elements base, prefix, infix, suffix, ending, addition. However it is divisible into two parts, each of which satisfies the second half of the definition. *Rough and ready* is a *complex word*.

Similarly, in

Ex. 6.19

The question of the Common Market has divided MPs *into three classes: the pro-marketeers; the anti-marketeers; and the schizophrenic*

prefix | base | suffix ending

pro-and-anti-marketeers

pro-and-anti- could be said to be a morpheme. It is acting as the element prefix in the structure of a word. However there is a sense in which *pro-* and *anti-* could be regarded as separate morphemes. Indeed we see each of them acting as such earlier in the example. *Pro-and-anti-* is one morpheme and yet divisible into two morphemes. It is a *complex morpheme*.

Complex units are sometimes called *unit-complexes*. Complex groups are sometimes called *group-complexes*, complex words are sometimes called *word-complexes* and complex morphemes are sometimes called *morpheme-complexes*.

An example has been given of a complex group, of a complex word and of a complex morpheme, but nothing has yet been said about a complex clause. A complex clause is really the same thing as a sentence. In fact sentences are sometimes called *complex clauses* or *clause-complexes*.

The sentence was included in the first section of this chapter since it is usually considered to be a basic unit of English grammar. But as far as its own structure is concerned it has much more in common with the complex units described in the second section of the chapter than it has with the other basic units of the first section.

The parts of a complex unit relate to each other in the same way as clauses relate to each other in the structure of a sentence. The relationship between *the men's halls* and *the women's halls* in Ex. 6.17, between *rough* and *ready* in Ex. 6.18, and between *pro-* and *anti-* in Ex. 6.19 is the same as that between *he huffed* and *he puffed* in Ex. 6.15. In each case the relationship is one of linkage or *co-ordination*. (We use the same Greek letters to symbolize the relationships between the parts of a complex unit as we do to symbolize the relationships between clauses in a sentence.)

Thus we could analyse Ex. 6.17, 6.18 and 6.19 as follows:

Ex. 6.17

Ex. 6.18

Ex. 6.19   ... *pro-and-anti-marketeers*

The relevant parts of their structural trees are shown in Figures 6.1, 6.2 and 6.3.

We say that the difference between the basic units on the one hand and the complex units, including the sentence, on the other hand is that the basic units have *multivariate* structures while the complex units have *univariate* structures.

FIGURE 6.1　　　*Part of Structural Tree of Ex. 6.17*

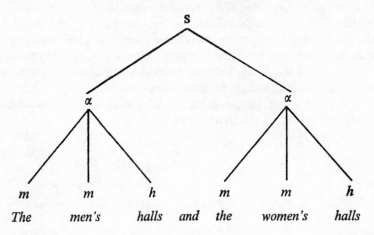

FIGURE 6.2　　　*Part of Structural Tree of Ex. 6.18*

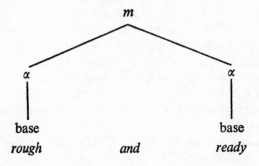

FIGURE 6.3　　　*Part of Structural Tree of Ex. 6.19*

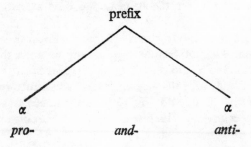

Multivariate structures are those in which there are different kinds of relationship between the different elements. In the S, P, C, A kind of structure for instance, the relationship between S and P is different from the relationship between C and P, which is different from the relationship between A and P, which is different from the relationship between S and C, which is different from the relationship between S and A, which is different from the relationship between C and A.

Univariate structures are those in which there is only one kind of relationship between the elements. In

Ex. 6.20

His hair, his beard, his skin and his clothes is a complex group with the structure α α α α. The relationship between the first α and the second α is the same as that between the first α and the third α, which is the same as that between the first α and the fourth α, which is the same as that between the second α and the third α, which is the same as that between the second α and the fourth α, which is the same as that between the third α and the fourth α. The elements are all co-ordinate with each other.

Univariate structures can be subdivided into *paratactic* univariate structures and *hypotactic* univariate structures.

All the examples of complex units given in this section of the chapter so far have been examples of paratactic univariate structures. In each of them the elements have been of equal status. The one kind of relationship existing between the elements has been a relationship of co-ordination.

Hypotactic univariate structures, like paratactic univariate structures, have only one kind of relationship existing between their elements, but in this case the relationship is one of *subordination*.

We have already seen that sentences can have structures involving a relationship of subordination. Ex. 6.14, for instance, has a hypotactic univariate structure since its first element is subordinate to its second element.

An example of a complex group with a hypotactic univariate structure is *Sandy MacTavish, from Glasgow*, in

$$
\begin{array}{c|c|c|c}
 & \text{S} & & \\
\alpha & & \beta & \\
\end{array}
$$

Ex. 6.21 | *Sandy MacTavish,* | *from Glasgow,* | *did not,*
to our surprise, have a Scottish accent.

An example of a complex word with a hypotactic univariate structure is *helpful, if dim*, in

$$
\begin{array}{cccc}
m & m & m & h \\
 & \alpha & \beta & \\
\end{array}
$$

Ex. 6.22 | *The helpful, if dim, new assistant.*

We have seen that the basic units, clause, group, word, have multivariate structures, while the complex units, including the sentence, have univariate structures. We have seen that there are two kinds of univariate structure: paratactic univariate structure and hypotactic univariate structure. Paratactic univariate structures can be subdivided yet again.

As well as the paratactic univariate structures involving a relationship of co-ordination, which have already been exemplified, there are paratactic univariate structures involving a relationship of *apposition*. In

$$
\begin{array}{c|c|c|c}
 & \text{S} & \text{P} & \text{C} \\
\alpha' & \alpha' & & \\
\end{array}
$$

Ex. 6.23 ‖ *That man,* ⦙ *Owen Evans,* | *is* | *a footballer* ‖

Owen Evans is equated with *that man* by being juxtaposed to it. *Owen Evans* is said to be in apposition to *that man*.

(The α α symbols indicate that, as in the case of a co-ordinate paratactic univariate structure, the elements of an appositional paratactic univariate structure are of equal status. The strokes after the αs differentiate the α elements of an appositional paratactic univariate structure from those of a co-ordinate paratactic univariate structure.)

Ex. 6.23 is an example of a complex group with appositional paratactic univariate structure. Some of the examples of the 'synonym habit', which Shakespeare mocks in *Love's Labour's Lost* (III, i, 130–1), may be said to be examples of complex words with appositional paratactic univariate structure.

$$
\begin{array}{c|ccccc}
a & & & v & & \\
 & \alpha' & \alpha' & & \alpha' & \alpha' \\
\end{array}
$$

Ex. 6.24 *thou* | *wert immured, restrained, captivated, bound.*

So far in this section of the chapter all the examples have been of stretches of language in whose structural trees complex units have alternated with basic units. However it is possible for successive layers of a structural tree to be occupied by the structures of complex units. In

Ex. 6.25 *She looked after the baby while I was visiting my son who was in hospital because he had to have an operation*

the β part of the sentence, *while I was visiting my son who was in hospital because he had to have an operation,* is subordinate to the α part of the sentence, *She looked after the baby.* Within the β part of the sentence there is another example of an αβ structure: *who was in hospital because he had to have an operation* is subordinate to *while I was visiting my son.* Within this second β element there is yet another example of an αβ structure: *because he had to have an operation* is subordinate to *who was in hospital.* The upper part of the structural tree of this sentence is shown in Figure 6.4.

FIGURE 6.4 *Part of Structural Tree of Ex. 6.25*

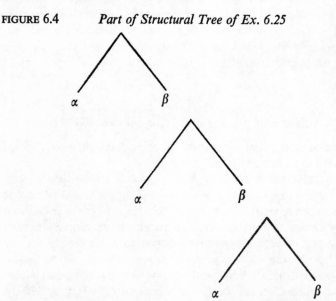

Ex. 6.25 is an example of hypotactic univariate structures occurring at successive layers in a structural tree. It is also possible for paratactic univariate structures to recur in this way. In

Ex. 6.26 *John and Mary and Peter and Susan went to 'The Sound of Music'* it is possible to assume that *John* and *Mary* and *Peter* and *Susan* are all equal items in the list and are equally co-ordinated, in which case *John and Mary and Peter and Susan* would be analysed like the complex group in Ex. 6.20. However it seems more probable that Ex. 6.26 is referring to two couples, John and Mary on the one hand and Peter and Susan on the other hand. In this case a more realistic analysis would be

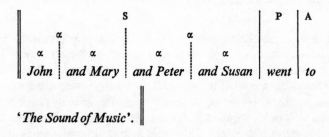

Part of the structural tree of this sentence is shown in Figure 6.5.

FIGURE 6.5 *Part of Structural Tree of Ex. 6.26*

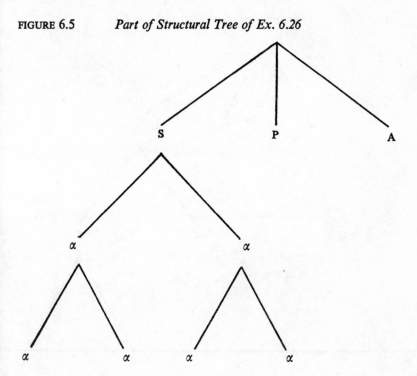

In

Ex. 6.27

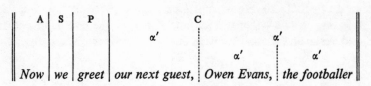

there is an example of a complex group in which appositional paratactic univariate structures occupy successive layers of the structural tree. Again it would be possible to assume that *our next guest, Owen Evans* and *the footballer* are all of equal status. But again it seems more realistic to assume that there are two layers of structure: initially *Owen Evans, the footballer* is being apposed to *our next guest* with a further apposition within the second element of the initial appositional structure (see Figure 6.6).

FIGURE 6.6   *Part of Structural Tree of Ex. 6.27*

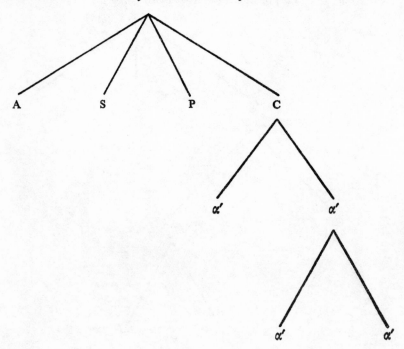

Since it is possible for univariate structures to recur in this way at successive layers of a structural tree, univariate structures are said to be *recursive* structures.

It should perhaps be said at this point that the analysis given earlier in the chapter for Ex. 6.15 can be improved upon since there are really two layers of structure where earlier only one was shown.

Ex. 6.15 ‖ *He huffed* ‖ *and he puffed,* ‖ *till he blew the house down.* ‖

Since the subject matter of Chapter 6 and the subject matter of Chapter 7 are so closely related, they will be discussed together in the Discussion section of Chapter 7.

7
Grammar: Rank

7.1 RANK

As was said in Chapter 6, units are of different sizes. We can arrange them on a scale in order of their size. This scale is known as the *rank* scale.

The simplest form of the rank scale for the English grammatical units is:

```
┌─sentence
├─clause
├─group
├─word
└─morpheme
```

A more complicated version would include the complex units:

```
┌─complex clause (clause-complex)
├─clause
├─complex group (group-complex)
├─group
├─complex word (word-complex)
├─word
├─complex morpheme (morpheme-complex)
└─morpheme
```

There are two ways of looking at the complex units. Either they can be seen as units in their own right, intermediate in size between the basic units, in which case the more complicated form of the rank scale given above is preferable. Or they can be seen as special cases of the basic units, each of the basic units being subdivisible into simple and complex versions of itself, in which case the simpler form of the rank scale is preferable. (It could of course be argued that the sentence should be removed from the simpler form of the rank scale since, if the second view of the complex units is accepted, then the sentence is merely a special case of the clause.) The term *unit-complex* perhaps implies the former of the two views of complex units, while the term *complex unit* perhaps implies the latter view. The latter view has been adopted by the writer of this book.

A rank scale, then, is a list of units arranged in order of their size. Like any other list of things arranged in order of size or status, it is a *hierarchy*.

A rank scale is a special kind of hierarchy in which the relationship between adjacent units is the same all the way down the scale.

In English, the relationship between sentences and clauses is the same as the relationship between clauses and groups, which is the same as the relationship between groups and words, which is the same as the relationship between words and morphemes.

This relationship is a 'consists of' relationship if one is thinking downwards along the scale, and a constituency relationship if one is thinking upwards along the scale. Each unit consists of members of the unit next below and each unit provides the constituents of the unit next above.

In English, sentences consist of clauses, clauses consist of groups, groups consist of words, and words consist of morphemes. Morphemes act as the constituents of words, words act as the constituents of groups, groups act as the constituents of clauses and clauses act as the constituents of sentences.

As has been said, each unit consists of members of the unit next below. Sometimes a unit consists of more than one member of the unit next below. Sometimes it consists of only one member of the unit next below.

		α		
S		**P**		**A**
m *h* *q*		*a* *v*		*p* *c*
base base ending base base		base(infix) base ending		base base
+ +		+		

Ex. 7.1 | The house s near by | were destroy ed | by fire.

This stretch of language is a sentence which consists of one clause. The clause consists of three groups. The first group consists of three words; the other two groups each consist of two words. The words *the*, *by* and *fire* each consist of one morpheme; the words *houses, nearby, were* and *destroyed* each consist of two morphemes.

Thus in this stretch of language the clause, the groups and four of the words each consist of more than one member of the unit next below, while the sentence and three of the words each consist of only one member of the unit next below.

Only whole units can act as the constituents of larger units. For instance, only whole groups can act as the constituents of clauses. A clause can consist of one whole group or of two (or more) whole groups, but cannot consist of just a part of a group or of one (or more) whole group(s) plus a part of a group.

(Since a unit can only consist of whole members of the unit next below we know that wherever there is a sentence boundary there must also be a clause boundary, that wherever there is a clause boundary there must also be a group boundary, that wherever there is a group boundary there must also be a word boundary, that wherever there is a word boundary there must also be a morpheme boundary. Where the boundaries of two or more units coincide in this way we only need to actually show the boundary of one of the units. The boundary that we show is that of the highest unit since the boundary of a higher unit implies the boundaries of lower units, whereas the boundary of a lower unit does not necessarily imply the boundaries of higher units.

In Ex. 7.1 the beginning of the sentence is also the beginning of a clause, the beginning of a group, the beginning of a word and the beginning of a morpheme. Only a sentence boundary is actually shown since this implies the boundaries of the lower units. No clause boundaries are shown at all for this example since the clause boundaries coincide with the sentence boundaries and are implied by the sentence boundaries.)

A unit cannot include among its constituents a unit of more than one rank below itself. For instance, a clause can include groups among its constituents but cannot include a member of a unit lower than the group. A clause can consist of two groups, but cannot consist of a group plus a word or a group plus a morpheme.

(Readers are warned that from now on this chapter delves rather deeply into a number of complexities of language and linguistics. Readers completely new to the subject may well prefer to move directly to Chapter 8, the chapter on systems, returning later for a further consideration of unit and rank. The system is after all the most important category of systemic linguistics and it could be said with truth that this book is taking rather a long time to get to this most important category!)

7.2 RANKSHIFT

It was stated in the last section that each unit consists of members of the unit next below. This perhaps implied that a unit cannot consist of anything other than members of the unit next below. Two other possibilities were in fact specifically ruled out: it was stated that a unit cannot include among its constituents a part of a unit or a unit of more than one rank below itself.

The statement that each unit consists of members of the unit next below is in general true. But it needs qualifying, since there are certain circumstances in which a unit can include among its constituents something other than a member of the unit next below. There are certain circumstances in which a unit can include among its constituents a unit of rank equal to or higher than itself.

Ex. 7.2   *The houses of historic interest were destroyed by fire.*

This is a sentence which consists of one clause. How many groups has the clause? When a class of students is asked this question, it usually happens that some people say there are three:

‖ *The houses of historic interest* | *were destroyed* | *by fire* ‖

while others say there are four:

‖ *The houses* | *of historic interest* | *were destroyed* | *by fire.* ‖

Both answers are right. The people who say three are remembering from Chapter 6 that a group is a stretch of language which acts as an s element, a P element, a C element or an A element in the structure of a clause. They are recognizing that *The houses of historic interest* is the subject of its clause, that *were destroyed* is the predicator, and that *by fire* is the adjunct. The people who say four are remembering that a group is a stretch of language which has a structure consisting of one or more of the elements *m, h, q*, or one or more of the elements *b, p, c*, or one or more of the elements *a, v, e*. They are recognizing that *of historic interest* has a preposition, *of*, and a completive, *historic interest*. The people who say three and the people who say four are both acknowledging certain properties which the language shows.

However, those who say three are more right than those who say four. The three groups, *The houses of historic interest*, *were destroyed*, and *by fire*, all fulfil the requirements of both halves of the definition of a group. Each of these three groups is acting as an S, P, C or A element and each has a structure consisting of one or more of the elements *m, h, q*, or one or more of the elements *b, p, c*, or one or more of the elements *a, v, e.*

	α	
S	P	A
m *h* *q*	*a* *v*	*p* *c*
The houses of historic interest	were destroyed	by fire.

The group, *of historic interest*, which those who say four consider to be the extra group, fulfils the requirement of one half of the definition in that it has the kind of structure that one expects of a group.

$$p \quad c$$
of historic interest

But it does not fulfil the requirement of the other half of the definition as it is not acting as an S, P, C or A element in the structure of a clause. It fulfils the requirement of half of the definition, but only half.

Of historic interest, then, fulfils the requirement of half of the definition of a group. It also fulfils the requirement of one half of the definition of a word. It is acting as one of the elements *m, h, q* or *b, p, c* or *a, v, e* in the structure of a group. It is acting as a qualifier, just like the single word *nearby* in Ex. 7.1.

		α	
	S	P	A
	m *h* *q*	*a* *v*	*p* *c*
Ex. 7.1	The houses nearby	were destroyed	by fire.
Ex. 7.2	The houses [of historic interest]	were destroyed	by fire.

Although *of historic interest* has the structure of a group rather than the structure of a word, it is acting just like a single word in the part it plays in the structure of another group.

Some readers may have been tempted to analyse *The houses of historic interest* as

$$* m \quad h \quad q \quad q \quad q$$
The houses of historic interest

but it should be pointed out that *of*, *historic* and *interest* are not separate qualifiers to *houses*. We are not talking about an 'of' kind of house or about an 'interest' kind of house. We are talking about a kind of house which is 'of historic interest'. *Of historic interest* as a whole qualifies *houses* but the individual bits of it do not. The single qualifier *of historic interest* can be contrasted with the four separate modifiers in

$$m \quad m \quad m \quad m \qquad h \qquad\qquad q$$

Ex. 7.3   *The ten old stone houses [of historic interest]*

Of historic interest as a whole describes and identifies *houses*, while *the, ten, old* and *stone* do so separately and individually.

Of historic interest, then, is half group, half word. We say that it is a group which has undergone *rankshift*. It is a group by virtue of its own structure, but in Ex. 7.2 it has in some respects shifted its rank to that of word and is functioning just as a single word would function.

We can say of both

Ex. 7.1   ‖ *The houses nearby* | *were destroyed* | *by fire* ‖

and

Ex. 7.2   ‖ *The houses [of historic interest]* | *were destroyed* | *by fire* ‖

that they are sentences which consist of a single clause, that the clause consists of three groups, that the first group consists of three 'words', and that the second and third groups each consist of two words. The only difference between the two sentences is that in the first sentence the third word of the first group really is a word, while in the second sentence the third 'word' of the first group is a group in disguise, a group acting as a word.

The houses nearby is a group which quite straightforwardly consists of members of the unit next below. *The houses [of historic interest]* is a group which includes among its constituents not only two members of the unit next below, but also a unit of rank equal to itself, the unit of equal rank having been rankshifted so as to act as a member of the unit next below.

Ex. 7.2, then, provides an example of a unit which includes among its constituents a unit of rank equal to itself. An example of a unit which includes among its constituents a unit of rank higher than itself is provided by Ex. 7.4.

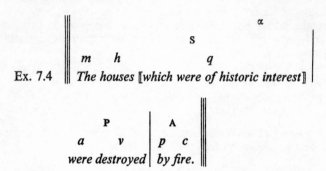

Ex. 7.4

In this sentence *which were of historic interest* is, from the point of view of its own structure, a clause. But it is functioning as a single word. Like *nearby* in Ex. 7.1 it is acting as the qualifier of the headword *houses*. It is a clause which has been rankshifted.

Ex. 7.4 has basically the same structure as Ex. 7.1 and Ex. 7.2. Like them it is a sentence which consists of a single clause. Like them its clause consists of three groups. Like them its first group has three constituents while the other two groups each have two. It differs from them in that the third constituent of the first group is neither a word nor a rankshifted group but a rankshifted clause.

The group *The houses* [[*which were of historic interest*]] includes among its constituents a clause, a unit of rank higher than itself, this higher unit having been rankshifted to act as if it were a word, the unit next below the group.

(Square brackets are used to mark a rankshifted unit. Single square brackets are used to mark a rankshifted group. Double square brackets, as shown above, are used to mark a rankshifted clause.)

Another way of talking about rankshift is by using the term *embedding*. We could say, for instance, that *which were of historic interest* is a clause embedded in the clause *The houses were destroyed by fire*.

It may be useful to consider some more examples of rankshift. In Chapter 5 two of the sentences used to provide examples of the *b, p, c* kind of structure were

Ex. 5.13   *Peter swam just beyond John*
Ex. 5.14   *He got nearly to France.*

Both these sentences are examples of stretches of language in which each unit straightforwardly consists of one or more of the unit next below.

If we compare with these two examples the example

Ex. 7.5 *John ran nearly to the end of the road*

we find that all three have basically the same structure:

				α		
	S	**P**			**A**	
	h	*v*	*b*	*p*		*c*
Ex. 5.13	*Peter*	*swam*	*just beyond*			*John*
Ex. 5.14	*He*	*got*	*nearly to*			*France*
Ex. 7.5	*John*	*ran*	*nearly to*	[*the end of the road*].		

The difference between them is that, whereas in each of Ex. 5.13 and Ex. 5.14 the completive is represented by a single word, in Ex. 7.5 the completive is represented by more than a single word. In Ex. 7.5 the completive is represented by *the end of the road*.

The end of the road is performing exactly the same function as the single words *John* and *France*. From the point of view of its function, it could be regarded as a word. However it has the kind of structure which we associate with a group:

$$m \quad h \quad q$$
the end of the road.

From the point of view of its own structure it is a group. *The end of the road* is a group which in Ex. 7.5 has been rankshifted to act as a word.

The group *nearly to* [*the end of the road*]

is another example of a unit which includes among its constituents a unit of rank equal to itself as well as two units of the rank next below.

The rankshifted group within *nearly to* [*the end of the road*] itself has a rankshifted group inside it. As has been shown above, *the end of the road* has the structure *mhq*. The modifier is represented by a single word *the* and the headword is represented by the single word *end*, but the qualifier is represented by a rankshifted group [*of the road*].

This rankshifted group within a rankshifted group has yet another rankshifted group within itself. *Of the road* has the structure

$$p \qquad c$$
of the road.

Its preposition is represented by a single word *of*, but its completive is represented by a rankshifted group [*the road*].

A more complete analysis of Ex. 7.5 than that given above would be

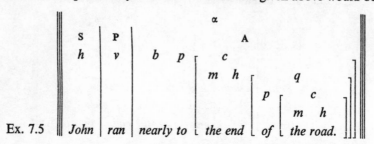

The relevant part of its structural tree is shown in Figure 7.1.

FIGURE 7.1　　　*Part of Structural Tree of Ex. 7.5*

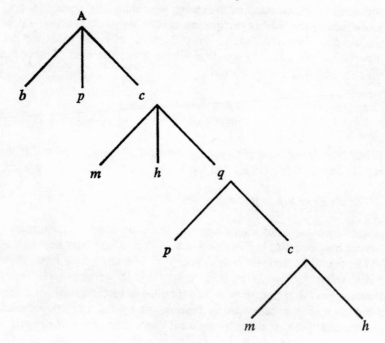

This arrangement of embedded groups, with alternating layers of the *b*, *p*, *c* kind of structure and the *m*, *h*, *q* kind of structure, is very common indeed in English.

A further example of rankshift is provided by

	α		
	S	P	C
Ex. 7.6	[[*That he would fail*]]	*was*	*inevitable.*

The subject of a clause is usually represented by a group. In this example the subject is being represented by a stretch of language which itself has the structure of a clause. [[*That he would fail*]] is a clause which in Ex. 7.6 has been rankshifted to act as a group. The clause [[*That he would fail*]] *was inevitable* includes among its constituents a unit of rank equal to itself.

The examples of rankshift given in this chapter are of some of the most common kinds of rankshift found in English. It should be noted however that other kinds of rankshift are also possible. An exhaustive list is beyond the scope of this book.

Rankshift, then, is the functioning of a formal item, which by virtue of its own structure is a member of one unit, as if it were a member of a lower unit. We have seen that through rankshift it is possible for a unit to include among its constituents a unit of rank equal to or higher than itself.

It was stated above that rankshift is the functioning of a stretch of language, which by virtue of its own structure is a member of one unit, as if it were a member of a *lower* unit. This point perhaps needs emphasizing. Rankshift is downward, not upward.

Some readers may perhaps be tempted to say of a stretch of language like *Do* in

Ex. 7.7   A   *Shall I close the door?*
       B   *Do.*

that *it is a word rankshifted upwards to act as a sentence. This is quite unnecessary. We can say all we want to about *Do* in terms of the original statement that a unit consists of one or more of the unit next below: *Do* is a sentence which consists of one clause; the clause consists of one group; the group consists of one word; the word consists of one morpheme. We do not need to resort to the concept of rankshift in order to explain the way in which *Do* is functioning.

Structures involving rankshift are potentially recursive. We could go on adding more and more layers of structure which would repeat the pattern already established.

There is already some recursion in Ex. 7.5. We could extend this still further. For example we might say

Ex. 7.8   *John ran nearly to [the end [of [the road*
            [along [the edge [of [the wood.]]]]]]]

This example is actually ambiguous. It is here taken as meaning 'John ran nearly to the end of the road, this road being the one along the edge of the wood' as opposed to 'John ran nearly to the end of the road; John ran along the edge of the wood' which would be analysed in a different way. For the second interpretation *nearly to the end of the road* and *along the edge of the wood* would be separate adjuncts, not parts of the same adjunct as for the first interpretation.

We could even say

Ex. 7.9   *John ran nearly to [the end [of [the road*
            [along [the edge [of [the wood [beside [the
            field [of barley]]]]]]]]]]]

meaning 'John ran nearly to the end of the road, this road being the one along the edge of the wood, this wood being the one beside the field of barley' as opposed to 'John ran nearly to the end of the road; John ran along the edge of the wood; John ran beside the field of barley'.

The relevant part of the structural tree of Ex. 7.9, given in Figure 7.2, shows the repeated patterning of the alternate layers of the *b, p, c* and the *m, h, q* kinds of structure.

Structures involving rankshift and structures involving complex units are in some ways alike. It is perhaps worthwhile at this point to compare them and to distinguish between them.

They are alike in that each provides cases of a unit including among its constituents something other than a member of the unit next below.

As we have seen in this chapter the group *The houses [of historic interest]* in Ex. 7.2 includes among its constituents another group, a unit of rank equal to itself. As we saw in Chapter 6, the group *The men's halls | and the women's halls* in Ex. 6.17 has as its constituents other groups, units of rank equal to itself.

However these two kinds of structure differ in that, whereas a unit containing a rankshifted unit can contain either a unit of equal rank or a unit of higher rank than itself, a complex unit always consists of units equal in rank to itself.

They also differ in that, whereas a unit containing a rankshifted unit can consist of a mixture of units of rank next below it and units of equal or higher rank, a complex unit always consists only of units of rank equal to itself.

FIGURE 7.2   *Part of Structural Tree of Ex. 7.9*

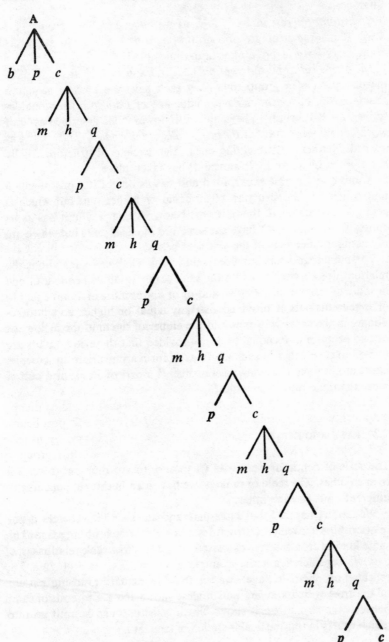

There is a third difference which is perhaps the most important of the differences.

Of historic interest in Ex. 7.2 is, as we have seen, half group, half word. It has the structure of a group but is acting as a word. In this example, *of historic interest* has been rankshifted.

The men's halls and *the women's halls* in Ex. 6.17 each satisfy half of the definition of a group since they each have the kind of structure characteristic of a group. Each could, like *of historic interest*, be described as 'half group'. They could not, however, be described as 'half word'. In no sense is either *the men's halls* or *the women's halls* acting as a word. Neither is representing one of the elements of structure usually represented by a word. No rankshift has taken place.

A unit containing a rankshifted unit has as one of its constituents a unit which has the structure of an equal or higher unit but which is acting as a member of the unit next below. A complex unit has as its constituents units which have the structure of equal units but which are not acting as members of the unit next below.

To summarize what has been said in this chapter so far about the relationships between units on the rank scale: a unit can consist of one or more of the unit next below, and/or of one or more of a unit equal to or higher than itself provided that any equal or higher unit is functioning in the same way as would a member of the unit next below, or of two or more units equal to itself provided that these equal units are related to each other in such a way as to form a univariate structure; a unit can not include among its constituents a part of a unit or a unit of more than one rank below itself.

7.3 RANK AND DEPTH

The scale of depth, as we saw in Chapter 5, relates different structures to each other. The scale of rank, as we have seen in this chapter, relates different units to each other.

We saw in Chapter 5 that a tree-diagram can be used to show the depth relationships between the structures of a given stretch of language. The same kind of tree-diagram can also be used to show rank relationships.

If we consider again the example given in Chapter 5 (Figure 5.3, repeated on opposite page), we see that the actual branching pattern of the tree, with its layers and nodes, shows the depth relationships between the structures; it shows which structures can be split up into which others in this particular stretch of language.

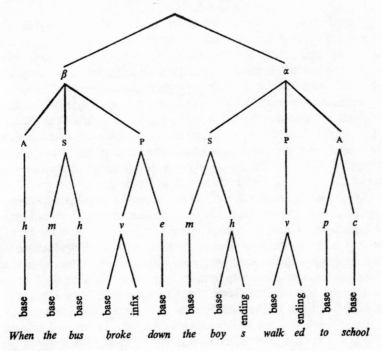

FIGURE 5.3   *Structural Tree of Ex. 5.52 (repeat)*

The fact that different kinds of symbol are used for the structures of different units (Greek letters for sentence structure, capital letters for clause structure, etc.) enables us also to see from the diagram the rank relationships between the units. We can see that in this example the sentence consists of clauses, the clauses consist of groups, the groups consist of words, and the words consist of morphemes.

In the structural tree of Ex. 5.52 the scales of rank and depth coincide. Each time we move down a layer on the scale of depth, we are also moving down one step on the scale of rank. This is shown by the fact that each kind of symbol occupies only one layer of the structural tree: Greek letters occupy only one layer, capital letters occupy only one layer, lower case letters occupy only one layer, terms written out in full occupy only one layer. Moreover the symbols occur in the order in which we should expect them to occur; since we know that the sentence is at the top of the rank scale, followed by the clause, followed by the group, followed by the word, followed by the morpheme, we should expect the highest kind of symbol on the structural tree to be Greek letters, followed by capital letters, followed by lower case letters, followed by terms written out in full.

These facts apply to the structural tree of Ex. 5.52 but they do not by any means apply to the structural trees of all stretches of language. In the structural tree of any stretch of language involving a complex unit and in the structural tree of any stretch of language involving rankshift, the two scales will not coincide. In the structural trees of stretches of language such as these, it is possible to move down a layer on the scale of depth without also moving down a step on the scale of rank. This is shown by the fact that a particular kind of symbol occupies more than one layer of a structural tree. In the structural trees of stretches of language such as these, the symbols may not occur in the order in which they occur in the structural tree of Ex. 5.52.

As we saw in Chapter 6, Ex. 6.17 is a stretch of language involving a complex unit. The left-hand side of its structural tree, given in Figure 7.3, shows the Greek letter kind of symbol occurring below the capital letter kind of symbol as well as above it. This is a case in which we do not have a straightforward progression from Greek letters to capital letters to lower case letters to terms written out in full. Greek letters are occupying more than one layer of the structural tree. At one point on the left-hand side of the structural tree we move down a layer on the scale of depth without also moving down a step on the scale of rank. We move down a layer from the layer which shows the SPA structure of the clause without arriving at a layer which shows the structure of a group. (It is not until we move down a further layer that we arrive at a layer showing group structure.) At this point the scales of rank and depth do not coincide.

If we were working with the more complicated version of the rank scale, on which complex units are treated as units in their own right, a different line of reasoning would of course be necessary here.

The adjunct of this example, *on* [*different sides* [*of* [*the campus*]]], is a stretch of language involving the kind of rankshift which allows a unit to include among its constituents a unit of rank equal to itself. This kind of rankshift does in fact occur three times in this example since the main group includes a rankshifted group which includes a rankshifted group which includes a rankshifted group. On the right-hand side of the structural tree there are four successive layers of lower case letters, one for the main group and one for each of the rankshifted groups. Again we have an instance of one kind of symbol occupying more than one

FIGURE 7.3   *Structural Tree of Ex. 6.17*

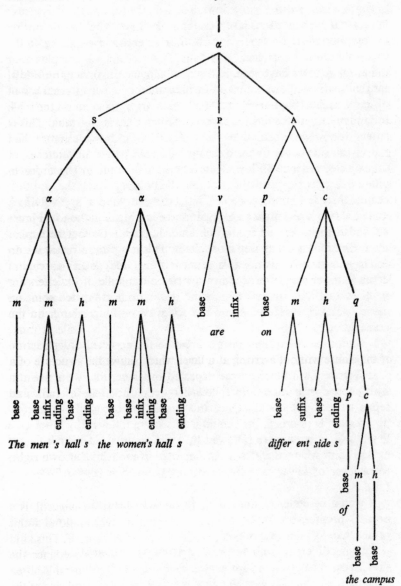

layer of the structural tree. Again we move down a layer on the scale of depth without also moving down a step on the scale of rank. We have in fact to move down four layers on the scale of depth before completing the one step move on the scale of rank from group to word. Again the two scales do not coincide.

Ex. 7.4 is, as we have seen, a stretch of language involving the kind of rankshift which allows a unit to include among its constituents a unit of rank higher than itself. Its structural tree, given in Figure 7.4, follows in its upper layers the expected order of kinds of symbol: Greek letters, followed by capital letters, followed by lower case letters. The right-hand side of the tree and the far left of the tree continue to follow the expected order as the lower case letters are followed by terms written out in full. However just left of centre, the point at which the rankshift occurs, there is a jump back to capital letters, the kind of symbol which was used two layers higher up. Again there is a break in the usual order of kinds of symbol and again one kind of symbol (in fact here more than one kind) is occupying more than one layer of the structural tree. Again we see that it is possible to move down a layer on the scale of depth without also moving down a step on the scale of rank. At one point in this tree, instead of moving down from group to word, we move back up to clause. Again the scales of rank and depth do not coincide.

It should be noted that, once a break in the expected order of symbols has occurred, the expected order is then resumed.

In Figure 7.4 a break in the expected order occurs at the point at which lower case letters are followed by capital letters instead of by terms written out in full. Once this break has occurred the normal progression is resumed, the capital letters being followed by lower case letters which in turn are followed by terms written out in full (except at one point where there is a further case of rankshift and where an extra layer of lower case letters occurs before the layer of terms in full).

It would be better in some ways to think in terms of a delay in the normal progression, or as a loop-back in the normal progression, rather than as an actual break.

By using different symbols for the structures of different units we can, then, show rank relationships as well as depth relationships on a structural tree. We can also show at which points the scales of rank and depth coincide and at which points they diverge.

The scales of rank and depth are very closely related since the categories with which they are concerned, unit and structure, are so closely

FIGURE 7.4   *Structural Tree of Ex. 7.4*

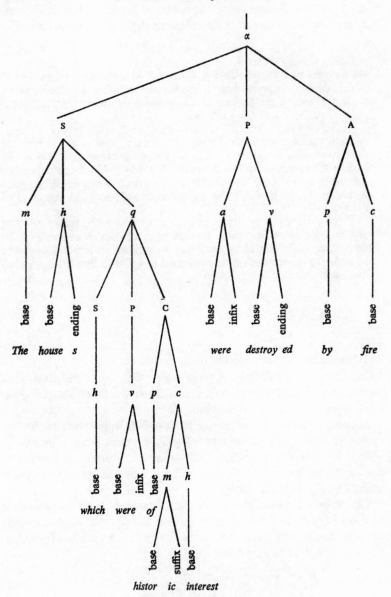

related. (In Chapter 6 the units were actually defined in terms of structures.) However we have seen that rank and depth are not exactly the same and that although they often coincide they do not always do so.

There are two ways of relating the scale of rank to the scale of depth.
Either we can follow the procedure adopted in this book. That is, we can assume that a stretch of language as a whole has depth, which can be expressed in terms of the number of layers in its structural tree. Then we can note how many of these layers are occupied by each unit of the rankscale.

Or we can start with the scale of rank and assign layers of depth to each unit on the scale. In this latter case, instead of numbering the layers of a structural tree from top to bottom as was done in Figure 5.4, we should begin again with Layer No 1 each time we moved to a new unit. The layers of the structural tree in Figure 5.4 would in fact all be Layer No 1 since each unit only has one layer of depth.

The former of these two approaches is perhaps the more useful at any rate for some purposes, since it gives an overall measure of the complexity of a stretch of language as well as an indication of the complexity at each rank of unit. It is for this reason that this approach had been adopted for this book.

7.4 DISCUSSION

7.4.1 *General Linguistics*

At the beginning of Chapter 6, units were defined as 'different sizes of formal items'. We should perhaps consider in more detail what is meant by the word *size* in this connection.

In some respects the word can be taken literally. Usually, for instance, a clause will literally be of greater extent than a group: in spoken English a clause will usually occupy a greater length of time than a group; in written English a clause will usually take up more space along the lines of a page.

This is by no means always the case, however. A clause can never of course be smaller than its own groups, the groups which act as its constituents, but a clause can be smaller than the groups of a neighbouring clause. In the sentence

	α		β		
	P	A	S	P	
	v	h	h	v	
Ex. 7.10	Go,	whenever	you	can	

the first clause *Go* takes up a smaller amount of space than *whenever* which is a group belonging to the second clause. It is also smaller than the group *you* and smaller than the group *can*. And in any example of a unit which consists of only one member of the unit next below, the upper unit will be the same size as the lower unit. The clause *Go* in Ex. 7.10 consists of only one group. The clause is the same size as the group of which it consists.

If, then, we say that a unit is a set of formal items which are alike in their size, we do partly mean size, in the sense of extent, but only partly. There is also another kind of likeness involved, a kind of likeness which is much more important than likeness in extent, a kind of likeness which is shared by clauses like *Go* as well as by clauses of a more usual sort which share the likeness of being of greater extent than groups. This other kind of likeness we could perhaps call likeness in status.

We saw in Section 5.3 that in order to arrive at the structures of a stretch of language and in order to show how these structures fitted together, it was necessary to make a series of cuts in the stretch of language. What we were really doing was to split the stretch of language up into formal items of different size. We then went on to arrange the structures of the stretch of language on a structural tree in order to show their relative depths; that is, in order to show the order in which the different structures had been arrived at in the cutting process. By implication we were also arranging on a scale the formal items which carried the structures and which represented elements of the structures; that is, by implication we were also indicating that the different formal items, like their structures, had been arrived at in a particular order in the cutting process.

Certain formal items are more likely to appear at certain stages of the cutting process than others. We can in fact divide the formal items of a language into sets according to the stages of the cutting process at which they are likely to appear. This is really what we mean by a unit. A unit is a set of formal items which are alike in their potentiality for appearing at a particular stage in the cutting process. This is the kind of likeness which was referred to above as likeness in status.

When we arrange the units of a language on a rank scale we are indicating what we think is their relative status; that is, we are indicating at what stages of the cutting process we expect the sets of formal items to appear relative to each other. The rank scale for English given at the beginning of the chapter indicates that formal items belonging to the unit clause can be expected to appear later in the cutting process than formal items belonging to the unit sentence but earlier in the cutting process than formal items belonging to the unit group; that formal items belonging to the unit group can be expected to appear later in the cutting process than formal items belonging to the unit clause but earlier in the cutting process than formal items belonging to the unit word; and that formal items belonging to the unit word can be expected to appear later in the cutting process than formal items belonging to the unit group but earlier in the cutting process than formal items belonging to the unit morpheme.

When discussing likeness in extent we had some difficulty in relating the first clause of Ex. 7.10 to other clauses. There is no difficulty over this example when we are discussing likeness in status. Since the unit clause comes immediately below the unit sentence on the rank scale, we should expect that the first set of cuts we make in a sentence would result in our having split the sentence into clauses. We make one cut in sentence Ex. 7.10 and we do indeed arrive at clauses: *Go* and *whenever you can*. In its status, *Go* is just like other clauses.

When considering units we are, then, primarily concerned with likeness in status of formal items rather than with likeness in extent, though the likeness in extent is usually associated with likeness in status.

Units also involve other kinds of likeness between formal items in addition to likeness in status and likeness in extent. Units, like structures and their elements, are the result of the interaction of a number of different kinds of pattern.

A unit, as was said in Chapter 6, can be identified by the part it plays in the structure of a larger unit. We are here taking into account what is essentially the same kind of likeness as the kind which was discussed in Section 5.2.3 under the heading of *Class*. Both in considering units and in considering classes we are concerned with likenesses between formal items in respect of the way in which they operate in the structures of larger formal items.

We also saw in Chapter 6 that a unit can be identified by its own structure. We are here taking into account what is essentially the same kind of likeness as the kind which was discussed in Section 5.2.4 under the heading of *Type*. Both in considering units and in considering types, we are concerned with likenesses between formal items in respect of their own structure.

The likenesses discussed here are not an exhaustive list of the kinds of likeness relevant to units. We shall see in Chapter 8 that units can be characterized not only by their status, by their extent, by the elements of structure which they represent and by the structures which they themselves carry, but also by the choices which they make.

When considering units, then, we need to be concerned with two of the kinds of likeness with which we were concerned when considering structures. However, we need to be concerned with them in a different way from the way in which we were concerned with them when considering structures. When considering units we are concerned with each of the two kinds of likeness at a more general level than when considering structures.

The likenesses between formal items which lead us to group them together as members of a unit are more general than the likenesses between formal items which lead us to group them together as members of a class; that is the likenesses are shared by a larger number of formal items. The formal items *scratched, just beyond John, the door, couldn't swim, nearly to France, operatic arias* all share the likenesses which lead us to say that they are members of the same unit, the unit that we call the group. Of these six formal items, only two, *scratched* and *couldn't swim*, share the likeness which leads us to say that they belong to the class of verbal group.

Similarly the likenesses between formal items which lead us to group them together as members of a unit are more general than (shared by a larger number of formal items than) the likenesses between formal items which lead us to group them together as members of a type. Of the six formal items listed in the previous paragraph as belonging to the unit group, again only two, *the door* and *operatic arias*, share the likeness which leads us to say that they belong to the *m, h, q* type of item.

From this point of view we can regard class and type as subdivisions of unit. *Scratched, just beyond John, the door, couldn't swim, quite quickly enough, operatic arias* are all members of the same unit, the group. They can be subdivided, as shown in Section 5.2.4 into three different classes: the verbal group, the adverbial group, the nominal group. They can also be subdivided, again as shown in Section 5.2.4, into three different types: *a, v, e* type, *b, p, c* type, *m, h, q* type.

The greater the generality of a likeness, the smaller the likeness itself is likely to be.

The likenesses which link together the members of a unit are smaller than the likenesses which link together the members of a class. All members of the unit group are alike in that they represent some element of the s, p, c, a kind of structure. All verbal groups are alike in that they represent one particular element, p, of the s, p, c, a kind of structure. We intuitively feel that a likeness which consists of a shared potentiality for representing one particular element is greater than a likeness which consists of a shared potentiality for representing any one of a number of elements.

Similarly the likenesses which link together the members of a unit are smaller than the likenesses which link together the members of a type. The analyses which have been given in this book of the various types of group suggest that all groups have something in common in their structure since each type of group has three elements possible in its structure. We could say, then, that all groups are alike in that they have the same number of elements possible in their structure. All *a*, *v*, *e* type groups are alike not only in that they have the same number of elements possible in their structure but also in that they have the same particular elements possible in their structure. The likenesses which link together the members of a type of group are greater than the likenesses which link together groups in general.

> Some linguists have analysed all types of group in terms of *m*, *h*, *q*, which indicates that they have seen greater likenesses between the different types of group than have been suggested here. Other linguists have given analyses which indicate that they do not see even as much similarity between the different types as has been suggested here.

Problems are sometimes caused by the fact that linguists would really like the likenesses they perceive to be both as general as possible and as great as possible at one and the same time. In the case we are discussing at the moment we can, as it were, have the bun and the ha'penny too. By making use of the category of unit as well as of the categories of class and type we can cater for a more general kind of likeness between formal items as well as for a greater kind of likeness.

> The two degrees of generality and the two degrees of greatness of likeness which have been discussed here are not of course the only degrees of generality and greatness of likeness which are relevant in linguistic analysis. Often it is necessary to cater for likenesses between formal items which are even less general (shared by even fewer formal items) and even greater than those which are catered for by class and type. For this purpose we can subdivide our classes and types into secondary classes and secondary types or subclasses and subtypes.

Because the category of unit is concerned with likenesses which are more general and less great than the likenesses with which other categories are concerned, making generalizations about units is easier and in some ways more satisfying than making generalizations about other categories. It is easier because the likenesses are less great, because we are making smaller demands on the likenesses we perceive. It is more satis-fying because the likenesses are more general, because generalizations which apply to a large number of items do seem more satisfying than those which apply only to a small number of items.

The generality of units and the generalizability of units make it possible to use the category of unit to talk both about likenesses in actuality between formal items and also about likenesses in potentiality between formal items.

In Chapter 5 we needed two different categories: structure, which enabled us to talk about likenesses between formal items in the way in which they were actually operating in given combinations of formal items; and class, which enabled us to talk about likenesses between for-mal items in their potentiality. It was shown in Section 5.2.3 that there could be a discrepancy between a formal item's potential (the way in which it was most likely to operate in combination with other formal items) and the way in which the formal item actually did operate in combination with the other formal items of a given stretch of language. At the degree of generality and the degree of greatness of likeness with which we were concerned in Chapter 5, it was necessary to have two distinct categories. However, since the likenesses with which unit is concerned are more general and less specific than those with which structure and class are concerned, there is not in the case of unit such a great discrepancy possible between actual and potential. There is not such a need therefore for two distinct categories, and we do in fact at this degree of generality use the one category unit both to talk about likenesses between formal items in the way in which they are actually operating in given stretches of language and also to talk about likenesses between formal items in their potentiality (likenesses, that is, in the way in which they are most likely to operate).

> This is why at some points in this section unit has been compared with structures and their elements while at other points unit has been compared with class and type. When we are thinking of units as sets of formal items actually operating in given stretches of language, then the comparisons with structures and their elements are the more relevant. When we are thinking of units as sets of items in a kind of reservoir of the resources of a language from which choices can be made, then comparisons with class and type are the more relevant.

Because of the generalizability of units, what discrepancy there is be-tween actual and potential can more easily be stated than in the case of the other categories; that is, it can more readily be reduced to a succinct set of rules. Such discrepancy has already been discussed in this chapter under the heading of *Rankshift*. When it was stated that a unit can consist of one or more of a unit equal to or higher than itself provided that any equal or higher unit is functioning in the same way as would a member of the unit next below, the possibilities for discrepancy between actual likenesses between formal items and potential likenesses between formal items were being reduced to a succinct set of rules.

Some further observations are necessary at this point on the difference between the scale of rank and the scale of depth and on the relationship between them.[1] It was shown in Section 7.3 that the two are distinct and do not always coincide, but the theoretical implications of their lack of coincidence have not yet been made clear.

It was stated at the beginning of Section 7.3 that the scale of depth relates structures to each other while the scale of rank relates units to each other. This is in fact an oversimplification of the true state of affairs since both rank and depth have connections with both structures and units.

By postulating a scale of depth we are implying that stretches of language can be split up into other stretches of language in a series of successive stages. In other words we are showing that formal items have a constituency relationship with each other. It is really formal items that are being related to each other by the scale of depth.

However it is also true that, as was said earlier, structures are related to each other by the scale of depth. The formal items represent elements of structure and carry structures. By relating the formal items to each other we are indirectly relating to each other the structures which the formal items represent and the structures which they carry. It should be stressed, however, that the relationship between structures is indirect. It is not strictly true to say that a structure can be split up into other structures. When we do say this, as in Section 5.3, we are really using a kind of shorthand. What we really mean is that an element of structure is represented by a formal item which can be split up into other formal items which are representing other elements of structure. (Structural tree-diagrams make it look as if the relationships between structures are direct relationships. Structural trees too are a kind of shorthand.)

As well as directly relating formal items and indirectly relating structures, the scale of depth also has links with unit. The most important

[1] It should be pointed out that Professor Halliday does not agree with the view of depth given in this book or with the suggested relationship between rank and depth. As stated in Chapter 2, the discussions of depth in this book are based on the views of Dr R. D. Huddleston (Huddleston 1965).

of the likenesses which lead us to group formal items into units and to arrange them on a rank scale is, as was shown earlier in this section, likeness in status; likeness, that is, in the formal item's potentiality for appearing at a particular stage in the cutting process; likeness, that is, in probable position on the scale of depth. The category of unit can thus be said to be derived from the scale of depth.

The scale of depth, then, is primarily concerned with relating formal items to each other. It also provides the basis for grouping the formal items into units. It also, indirectly, relates structures to each other.

Like the scale of depth, the scale of rank has links with formal items, with units and with structures.

However, with regard to formal items and units, the position for rank is the reverse of that for depth. Depth is primarily concerned with relating formal items to each other but has derivational links with units (since it provides the basis for units). Rank is primarily concerned with relating units to each other but has derivational links with formal items (since it is based on likenesses between formal items).

Another way of looking at this is to say that both rank and depth are ultimately concerned with relating the same things, formal items. But that rank is concerned with the formal items at a more general level than depth. Rank is not concerned with the formal items as individual formal items in the way that depth is concerned with them. Rank is concerned with the formal items as members of sets of items with shared likenesses in status.

Like depth, as well as having links with formal items and units, rank relates structures to each other. Like depth, it does so indirectly. Again, however, the relationships with which rank is concerned are at a more general level than those with which depth is concerned.

The scale of depth can be used to show, via the formal items, how the structures of a given stretch of language fit together. It can be used to show, for instance, that in one stretch of language an s element is represented by a formal item with the structure *mhq*. It can be used to show that in another stretch of language a c element is represented by a formal item with the structure *mmh*. It can be used to show that in another stretch of language an A element is represented by a formal item with the structure *pc*.

Descriptions such as those in the previous paragraph are all descriptions of particular stretches of language. We can make generalizations about such descriptions. We can group together structures such as *mhq*, *mmh* and *pc*, and show that they are alike in that they are all associated with (carried by) a particular set of formal items, a particular unit. We can also group together elements such as s, c and a, and show that they are alike in that they are all associated with (each forms part of a structure carried by) another particular set of formal items, another unit. The unit with which the *mhq*, *mmh* and *pc* structures are associated in this way is the group. The unit with which the elements s, c and a are associated is the clause. Since the group follows the clause on the rank scale, it is no surprise that in each of the descriptions of particular stretches of language given in the previous paragraph one of the elements s, c and a is represented by a formal item with one of the structures *mhq*, *mmh* and *pc*. It is possible to see a general pattern emerging from the particular descriptions. Not only can formal items be divided into sets according to their potentiality for appearing at particular stages in the cutting process. So too can structures.

The scale of depth relates individual formal items to each other in given stretches of language. In so doing it relates to each other the particular structures carried by the formal items. The scale of rank relates to each other sets of formal items with shared likenesses in status. In so doing it relates to each other the sets of structures associated with the sets of formal items, sets of structures which also have shared likenesses in status.

At first sight the insistence that structures can only be related to each other indirectly (via formal items at a less general level, via units at a more general level) may seem to be making things unnecessarily complicated, since we are taking two steps where one might have been thought to have been enough. However, individually each of the two steps will be considerably less complicated than would have been the one step had we tried to do in one step all that we wanted to do. By relating structures to each other via units or formal items instead of directly we have complicated the theory. But each stage of a description based on the theory will be less complicated as a result. This problem of balancing simplicity against complexity is a common one in linguistics. Language is extremely complex. No description of language can be both simple and adequate. It is unrealistic to hope for a simple description of language. It is much more a question of deciding at which points of one's theory or description to be simple and at which points to be complicated, recognizing that if one aims for greater simplicity at one point one will inevitably have to introduce compensatory complexity at another point. Often by complicating the theory it is possible to simplify descriptions. Some linguists have argued that the concepts of unit and rank are unnecessary, that they are needless complications of the theory. However systemic linguists have found them useful, since although they complicate the theory, they simplify certain problems of description.

Rank and depth, then, are related in that rank is a generalization from depth. They are alike in that both relate formal items to each other directly and in that both relate structures to each other indirectly. They differ in that, both in the case of formal items and in the case of structures, the relationships with which rank is concerned are more general than the relationships with which depth is concerned.

As a result of being more general, the relationships with which rank is concerned are more generalizable than those with which depth is concerned. This means that on the basis of rank we can say more about a particular language as a whole or about language in general than we can say on the basis of depth.

As has been said, the scale of depth is mainly concerned with relating particular formal items and particular structures in particular stretches of language. The theoretical implication of the scale of depth for language in general is simply that formal items do have a constituency relationship with each other and that via the formal items so too do the structures. The implication of the scale of depth for a particular language such as English is simply that its formal items do have a constituency relationship with each other and that via its formal items so too do its structures.

By postulating a scale of rank in addition to a scale of depth we are suggesting that it is a characteristic of language in general, not only that there is a constituency relationship between formal items and between structures, but also that there is some regularity about this constituency relationship. We are suggesting that both the formal items and the structures can be divided into sets and that it is possible to predict which sets will provide the constituents for which other sets. When describing a particular language, by postulating a rank scale for that language, we are able to suggest not only that there is a constituency relationship between formal items and between the structures, but also that there is regularity and predictability in this constituency relationship. We can in fact specify the rules which constitute the regularity and which form the basis for the predictability. The rules which govern the constituency relationships between the units (sets of formal items) of English are summarized at the end of Section 7.2. These rules, together with the actual rank scale for English shown at the beginning of the chapter, form the basis for any predictions we wish to make about constituency relationships between English formal items. Via these rules for English units we can arrive at a similar set of rules for English structures which will enable us to make predictions about the way in which the structures will be fitting together in any stretch of English—in any stretch of

English not yet spoken or written, as well as in any stretch of English with which we are already familiar.

By means of the rank scale, then, we can not only make the somewhat vague general statement that in language in general or in a particular language the formal items and the structures fit together. We can also show that there is regularity and predictability in the ways in which they fit together. For a particular language we can specify these ways with some precision.

We now return to the question of the significance of lack of coincidence of rank and depth in the structural tree of a stretch of language, as exemplified in Section 7.3. We are here really back again to talking about discrepancy between actual and potential (potential in the sense of what is most likely). When, in a stretch of language, the formal items actually have the constituency relationships which are potentially associated with them (when they have the constituency relationships that they are most likely to have), then the scales of rank and depth do coincide, step by step, in the structural tree. It is only when there is a discrepancy between actual and most typical potential that we find in a structural tree lack of coincidence of the two scales.

The possibility of discrepancy between actual and most typical potential may perhaps seem to contradict what has just been said about the regularity and predictability of constituency relationships. Instances of rankshift may seem to be exceptions to the rules which have been said to exist. And indeed they are exceptions to the most general rules. But they are exceptions which are themselves rule-governed. As has already been pointed out, it is relatively easy to reduce to a succinct set of statements the rules that govern them.

It should be noted that lack of coincidence between rank and depth is one-way only. It is possible to move down a step on the scale of depth without also moving down a step on the scale of rank. It is not possible to move down a step on the scale of rank without also moving down a step on the scale of depth.

It is perhaps too fanciful to suggest an analogy between depth and rank on the one hand and the metre and rhythm of verse on the other hand. For any stretch of language, depth like metre proceeds with complete regularity step by step. Rank like rhythm is superimposed on depth, providing the irregularity, the rise and fall, the light and shade. In certain forms of language rank and depth tend to coincide, just as in doggerel forms of verse metre and rhythm tend to coincide. In certain other forms of language (the more elegant? the more poetic?) rank and depth tend not to coincide. This is not to decry the 'doggerel' forms of language. For certain purposes they are more effective than the more 'poetic' forms of language, as they tend to be simpler and clearer, just as doggerel is occasionally more effective than poetry—as for example when the verse is being used as a mnemonic.

Chapter 5's contribution to answers to the questions: What is language? and How does language work? was an exploration of the idea that at the level of grammar language is a patterned phenomenon, the patterns providing the regularity which is necessary for the working of language. Chapters 6 and 7 have continued the exploration of the patterning. They have been particularly concerned with the ways in which formal items and their patterns fit together in language. They have shown that there is pattern and regularity in the fitting together as well as in the basic patterns themselves.

All languages can be shown to have units. For every language the units can be arranged on a rank scale. It is not theoretically necessary for all languages to have exactly the same units, but in fact all the languages so far examined from this point of view do seem to show similarity in their units. It may be that the category of unit is general in this sense also. It may be that not only does a particular unit link a large number of formal items within a particular language, it is perhaps general also in that it is applicable to a large number of different languages.

7.4.2 *Descriptive Linguistics*

The generalizability of units makes them a useful starting point in the description of language. Certainly one would not achieve a very penetrating description if one remained at this very general level for too long. But on the other hand if one jumps straight into considerations of very specific likenesses at the beginning of a description one risks not being able to see the wood for the trees. Units can provide a starting point for a description and also a framework for the finer distinctions which follow. We shall see in Chapter 8 that, in particular, units provide a useful starting point for the discussion of systems.

Another thing that makes the category of unit useful in descriptions of language is the fact that it is interrelated with so many other categories. It is related to structure in two different ways since units represent elements of structure and also carry structures. It is taxonomically related to class and type, class and type being different kinds of subdivision of unit. As will be seen in the following chapters, it is related to system in two different ways. It is a corner at which the dimensions of a multi-dimensional analysis meet. As such it is useful as a mapping device; that is, it is useful as a way of correlating the other categories, of showing how far there is a correspondence between them. We can, as it were, use a unit as if it were an outline map of a country on which we mark population patterns, communication patterns, physical relief patterns and patterns of climate in order to show how far there is a correspondence between these different kinds of pattern. Via unit we can relate to each other the different aspects of a description.

Description of language can be large-scale or small-scale. It can be description of whole languages or whole varieties of languages, or it can be description of particular stretches of language. Usually the large-scale descriptions are built up from small-scale descriptions. The following paragraphs apply primarily to small-scale descriptions, but since small-scale descriptions usually contribute to large-scale descriptions, the paragraphs are relevant also to large-scale descriptions.

It was stated in Chapter 5 that in order to fully describe a stretch of language it is necessary to consider the stretch of language in relation to all the possible kinds of structure in the language. It is equally true to say that in order to fully describe a stretch of language it is necessary to consider the stretch of language in relation to all the units of the language.

If we are to fully describe *Do* in Ex. 7.7.

Ex. 7.7   A   *Shall I close the door?*
          B   *Do.*

it is not sufficient to say just that *Do* is a word or to say just that *Do* is a sentence, or even to say that *Do* is a sentence which consists of one word. We must say that *Do* is a sentence which consists of one clause which consists of one group which consists of one word which consists of one morpheme.

From the point of view of the structure of the stretch of language this may seem rather pedantic. We do learn something about the structure of the stretch of language by describing it in this way, but, admittedly, what we learn is not very much.

However, as has been said, we shall see in Chapter 8 that a unit is characterized not only by the structures which it carries and which it represents but also by the choices which it makes. At a later stage in the analysis we shall want to show that *Do* is like other, perhaps more obvious, sentences in the choices it has made. We shall want to show that *Do* is like other, perhaps more obvious, clauses in the choices it has made. We shall want to show that *Do* is like other, perhaps more obvious, groups in the choices it has made. We shall also want to show that *Do* is like other words and like other morphemes in its choices. *Do* has made choices at every rank of unit. In order to describe its choices it will be necessary to consider it as each unit in turn.

As shown in Chapter 6, each unit is defined in terms of its relation to the unit above it and the unit below it on the rank scale. This means that when one is analysing a stretch of language one cannot recognize the members of any unit until one has also tried to identify the members of the units above and below.

One cannot recognize English groups until one has tried to identify the clauses of which they are the constituents and the words of which they consist. And of course identifying the clauses involves the consideration of sentences, and identifying the words involves the consideration of morphemes.

What one has to do is to *shunt*; that is, to move backwards and forwards along the rank scale looking for clues until the total pattern emerges.

Analysing a passage into units is rather like doing a crossword. One guesses 1 down of a crossword and tentatively writes in the answer. This provides one with letters which act as clues to 1 across, 8 across and 10 across. If one cannot think of anything for 1 across, 8 across or 10 across which will fit with one's answer to 1 down, one has to consider the possibility that one's answer to 1 down was wrong. One goes backwards and forwards, up and down through the crossword until one has completed it. One cannot be sure that one's early answers were correct until one has finished the crossword and seen if every answer fits with every other answer.

When one is analysing a stretch of language into units, one sees a unit that one thinks one recognizes and one makes a tentative mental note of it. This provides one with clues to the identification of other units. If one's later identifications do not fit with one's earliest impression, one has to consider the possibility that one's earliest impression was unsatisfactory. One goes backwards and forwards along the rank scale until one has completed the analysis. One cannot be sure that one's early identifications were satisfactory until one has finished the analysis and seen if every identification fits with every other identification.

When analysing a passage of English, then, one cannot first identify the sentences in isolation and then move on to the clauses and then to the other units in turn down the scale, and nor can one begin with morphemes and work up to sentences. However, for clarity of presentation, when one is writing up one's analysis one often pretends that one has moved just in one direction or the other. Even in the actual analysis one can focus on each unit in turn, as long as one realizes that one cannot actually identify the members of the focal unit unless one shunts along the rank scale.

It was stated in Chapter 5 that, owing to the very great complexity of language, different descriptions were possible for the same stretch of language when the structures of the stretch of language were being considered. It is equally true when units are being considered that different descriptions are possible for the same stretch of language.

One borderline which is very difficult to draw is the borderline between hypotactic univariate structures and structures involving a rankshifted unit.

In Chapter 6, Ex. 6.14 was treated as a hypotactic univariate structure:

Ex. 6.14 ‖ *β* ‖ *α* ‖
‖ *When night came,* ‖ *he was far from home.* ‖

The example was thus analysed as a sentence (or a complex clause) consisting of two separate clauses. Some linguists would argue, however, that it should be treated differently. They would argue that *When night came* is really acting as an adjunct and that it is therefore not a separate clause but a rankshifted clause within the main clause:

Ex. 6.14 ‖ *α* ‖
‖ A | S | P | A ‖
‖ ⟦*When night came,*⟧ | *he* | *was* | *far from home.* ‖

Some linguists would in fact regard all subordinate clauses as rankshifted, thereby virtually abolishing the distinction between hypotactic univariate structures and structures involving rankshift, abolishing it at any rate at this rank.

It is however a useful distinction to retain, in spite of the difficulty in drawing the borderline, since it allows the analysis to show a difference between such an example as

Ex. 7.4 *The houses which were of historic interest were destroyed by fire*

and such an example as

Ex. 7.11 *The houses, which were of historic interest, were destroyed by fire.*

The two examples are written differently in that the second has two commas while the first does not, they would be spoken differently, and they differ in meaning. In the first example, *which were of historic interest* is being used to actually identify the houses in question, to explain which houses were destroyed by fire. In the second example it is assumed that the reader already knows which houses are being discussed. In this example *which were of historic interest* is being used simply to give an additional piece of information about the houses.

In the terminology of traditional grammars *which were of historic interest* is, in Ex. 7.4, a *defining* or *restrictive* clause while in Ex. 7.11 it is a *non-defining* or *non-restrictive* clause.

Another pair of examples which show the same distinction are:

Ex. 7.12   *My wife who lives in Rio de Janeiro sent me a Christmas card*

Ex. 7.13   *My wife, who lives in Rio de Janeiro, sent me a Christmas card.*

The author of the first sentence has a number of wives and *who lives in Rio de Janeiro* is being used to identify the one who sent the card. The author of the second sentence has only one wife and *who lives in Rio de Janeiro* is used simply to give an additional piece of information about her.

Since in each pair the second example differs in meaning from the first, it is fitting that in each pair the second example should be given a different grammatical description from the first. In each pair the first example is an example of a stretch of language with a structure involving rankshift. In each pair the second example is an example of a complex clause with hypotactic univariate structure.

In the first example of each pair, *which were of historic interest* and *who lives in Rio de Janeiro* are each an integral part of the group which is acting as an s element. Each is a clause which has been rankshifted to act like a word. In the second example of each pair, *which were of historic interest* and *who lives in Rio de Janeiro* are not integral parts of s elements. They are quite separate clauses, though each is dependent on and occurs in the middle of another clause, see illustration overleaf.

(Double round brackets indicate an *included* clause, a clause which occurs in the middle of another clause, but which is not an integral part of another clause in the way in which a rankshifted clause is part of another clause.)

	s		P		A
	m	h	a	v	p	c

Ex. 7.4   The houses [which were of historic interest] | were destroyed | by fire

α
β

Ex. 7.11   The houses, (which were of historic interest,) were destroyed   by fire

α

	s		P	C		C
	m	h	v	h	m	m

Ex. 7.12   My wife [who lives in Rio de Janeiro] | sent | me | a Christmas card

α
β

Ex. 7.13   My wife, (who lives in Rio de Janeiro,) sent   me   a Christmas card

7.4.3   Contrastive Linguistics

It was suggested in Chapter 5 that the scale of depth could be used as a measure of complexity and that, on the basis of the number of layers and the number of nodes per layer in their structural trees, stretches of language could be compared and contrasted. The scale of rank can be used to make finer comparisons and contrasts of this kind.

It may well happen that two stretches of language are alike in their overall complexity in that they have the same number of layers and the same average number of nodes per layer in their structural trees. By reference to the scale of depth we could show the similarity between them. But it may well be that although they are alike, they are not exactly alike. They may differ in the precise points at which they are complex and the precise points at which they are simple. One stretch of language may be complex at the rank of sentence to clause, taking a number of layers of depth to move down this one rank of unit, but simple at the lower ranks. The other stretch of language may be simple at the higher ranks but complex at the rank of word to morpheme. By superimposing the scale of rank on the scale of depth we could pinpoint the differences between the two stretches of language.

When contrasting two idiolects we may find that one person has a tendency to be complex at one rank of unit while the other person has a tendency to be complex at another rank of unit. (If someone has a tendency to be complex at all ranks we begin to feel the need to use what has been called 'the fog index'!)

Similar tendencies can be observed when contrasting different registers.

Even whole languages can be contrasted in this way. German, for instance, tends to be more complex at the rank of word to morpheme than English.

The notion of differing degrees of complexity of language is itself a complex notion. It should not be thought that the kind of complexity discussed here is the only kind of complexity worth measuring nor that the way of measuring it suggested here is the only way of measuring it.

7.4.4   Applied Linguistics

As was indicated in Chapter 5, those concerned with the teaching of English to children have shown interest in the extent to which children's language becomes more complex with age. By contrasting the language of different age groups in the way suggested in Section 7.4.3 we could pinpoint some of the developments which take place.

Another application of the concepts of unit and rank which has relevance to language teaching is that of J. C. Catford who uses the concepts to distinguish between different kinds of translation (Catford, 1965).

These concepts can, again, be used to discuss certain kinds of literary patterning. One brief example of this may be given.

Readers of Bacon's essay, *Of Studies*, will have noticed the pattern of threes which runs through the essay. Time and again, three stretches of language of similar structure are juxtaposed to each other and made to balance each other. What may not be so immediately obvious is that the pattern includes a progression up the rank scale. In the first sentence three groups are linked together, in the second sentence three clauses balance each other, and towards the end of the essay three sentences of similar structure are juxtaposed. The pattern in the middle of the essay for the most part consists of variations on the clause theme. The last sentence of the Bacon essay is a simple sentence, consisting of only one clause. This, coming after a succession of complex sentences, makes a firm ending.

Since the most fundamental aspects of language have not yet been discussed in this book, it is not yet possible to do more than suggest just a few fairly simple and elementary applications of this kind of linguistics.

7.4.5 *Systemic Linguistics and Other Schools of Linguistics*

Systemic linguistics is not alone in recognizing the concepts of unit and rank. It does, however, differ from some other schools of linguistics in the importance which it attaches to these concepts. Some aspects of unit and rank, particularly rank, have aroused a certain amount of controversy. Reference is made in the bibliography to papers relevant to the controversy.

It was stated in Chapter 2 that the schools of linguistics with which systemic linguistics has most in common are stratificational grammar and tagmemics. It is perhaps worth noting here that one of the things which these three schools have in common is that they all attach importance to the concepts of unit and rank.

8
Grammar: System

In Chapters 5, 6 and 7, the emphasis has been on the axis of chain rather than on the axis of choice. Occasionally matters relevant to the axis of choice have been discussed; whenever we have been considering matters such as class, whenever we have been considering potentiality rather than actuality, we have been concerned with the axis of choice rather than with the axis of chain. However in the main it is true to say that in Chapters 5, 6 and 7 the focus has been on the axis of chain.

Similarly, in Chapters 5, 6 and 7 the emphasis has been on the more surface aspects of grammar, on the forms of grammar, on the patterns of grammar and the way in which they fit together, rather than on the more fundamental aspects of grammar, the meanings of grammar. Occasionally matters relevant to the more fundamental aspects have been discussed; whenever we have been considering matters such as function, we have been concerned with the more fundamental aspects of grammar. However in the main it is true to say that in Chapters 5, 6 and 7 the focus has been on the more surface aspects of grammar.

In Chapters 8 and 9 there will be a twofold shift of emphasis. The focus will be on the axis of choice rather than on the axis of chain. The focus will be on the more fundamental aspects of grammar, on the meanings of grammar, rather than on the more surface aspects of grammar.

An attempt will be made in the second chapter of Volume II to show how these four corners of the systemic model of grammar fit together.

Chapters 8 and 9 of this volume and Chapter 2 of Volume II are the most important chapters of the book for an understanding of systemic grammar.

8.1 SYSTEMS

Systems are lists of choices which are available in the grammar of a language.

For instance in English there is a system of *number*, with the choice between *singular* and *plural*.

NUMBER ⟶ ┌─singular
          └─plural

There is a system of *person*, with the choice between *first*, *second* and *third*.

PERSON ⟶ ┌─first
         ├─second
         └─third

There is a system of *gender*, with the choice between *masculine*, *feminine* and *neuter*.

GENDER ⟶ ┌─masculine
         ├─feminine
         └─neuter

There is a system of *polarity*, with the choice between *positive* and *negative*.

POLARITY ⟶ ┌─positive
           └─negative

There is a system of *finiteness*, with the choice between *finite* and *non-finite*.

FINITENESS ⟶ ┌─finite
             └─non-finite

The terms *finite* and *non-finite* are being used here with the same meanings as they have in traditional grammars. For readers not familiar with traditional grammars it may be necessary to explain that *finite* means 'being limited in respect of such properties as person and number' while *non-finite* means 'not being limited in respect of such properties as person and number'. The choice between finite and non-finite applies to verbal groups (as opposed to nominal groups or adverbial groups). A verbal group which is finite has its person and number specified in its own clause, usually by a combination of its own form and the form of an accompanying nominal group. For example the verbal groups of (*I*) *am*, (*he*) *sees* and (*they*) *went* are all finite. A verbal group which is non-finite has its person and number left vague; there is nothing in its own form to specify person or number and usually there is nothing in an accompanying nominal group either. For example the verbal groups of *having finished* (*the course*), *to pass* (*the exam*) and (*if*) *prevented* are all non-finite.

There is a system of *tense*, with the choice between *past*, *present* and *future*.

There is a system of *mood*, with the choice between *declarative* (making a statement), *interrogative* (asking a question) and *imperative* (giving a command).

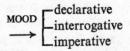

It must be stressed that the examples given above are only a few of the very many grammatical systems of English.

It should also be pointed out that the systems are really more complicated than the formulations of them given above make them appear. At this initial stage in the introduction of systems an attempt has been made to present them as simply as possible and also to refer to them as far as possible in the terms which are used for them in traditional grammars. More complex accounts of some systems will be given later in this chapter and in following chapters.

A system, then, is a list. It is a list of choices; that is, a list of things between which it is possible to choose. What are these 'things between which it is possible to choose'? They are *meanings*. They are meanings between which the grammar of a language is able to distinguish.

When we refer to something, we can choose either to mean one of that something or to mean more than one of that something. The grammar of English enables us to distinguish between singular and plural.

When we refer to an event, we can choose to mean that the event has already happened, or to mean that it is happening now, or to mean that it will be happening. The grammar of English enables us to distinguish between past, present and future.

When we speak of a person, we can choose to mean the person who is speaking at the time, or to mean the person who is being addressed, or to mean someone other than the two people involved in the conversation. The grammar of English enables us to distinguish between first person, second person and third person.

Readers are reminded that the questions of how far choice is conscious and how far choice is free were discussed in Chapter 4.

The items in a system are, then, distinct and distinguishable meanings. The technical name for these items is the *terms* in the system, although sometimes they are referred to as *options*. (The latter name for them emphasizes the fact that they are things between which choices are made.)

Although distinct, the terms of a particular system have something in common. They belong to the same area of meaning. Singular and plural are distinct but they both have to do with number. Past, present and future are distinct but they all have to do with time.

It is on the grounds of their common area of meaning that we group terms together in a system. Since singular and plural both have to do with number we can say that they belong to the same system. Since past, present and future all have to do with time we can say that they all belong to the same system. Singular and past do not have an area of meaning in common. They belong to different systems.

The terms in a system, then, are distinct meanings within a common area of meaning. By giving a name, such as *singular*, to a term, we are able to indicate something of the nature of that particular distinct meaning. By giving a name, such as *number*, to a system, we are able to indicate something of what its terms have in common.

8.2 THE ESSENTIAL PROPERTIES OF SYSTEMS

Systems have three essential characteristics:

(i) The terms in a system are mutually exclusive. The selection of one of the terms precludes the selection of any of the others.

For instance the two terms in the system of number are mutually exclusive. If something is singular, it cannot at the same time be plural. The selection of the singular term from the system precludes the selection of the plural term.

Similarly, if one is asking a question one cannot at the same time be making a statement or giving a command. The selection of interrogative from the system of mood precludes the selection of either declarative or imperative.

(ii) A system is finite. (The word *finite* is used here in its mathematical sense, not in the grammatical sense in which it was used earlier in the chapter, though of course the two senses have something in common.) It is possible to fix a limit for a system and to say that it consists of a certain countable number of terms, no more, no less. The limit is set in such a way that all the terms which are mutually exclusive with each other are included in the system, while any terms not mutually exclusive with those in the system are excluded from the system.

The system of polarity is finite. It consists of the two terms negative and positive and no others. The term negative is the only term which is mutually exclusive with the term positive. The system can therefore be said to contain all the terms which are mutually exclusive with each other. The system does not include any terms which are not mutually exclusive with the terms negative and positive. The term singular, for instance, is excluded from the system of polarity since it is not mutually exclusive with the terms negative and positive.

(iii) The meaning of each term in a system depends on the meaning of the other terms in the system. If the meaning of one of the terms in a system is changed, the meaning of other terms in the system will also change. If a term is added to a system or subtracted from a system, the meaning of other terms in the system will change.

Where present-day English has two terms in its number system, Old English had three terms: singular, dual and plural. The term plural had a different meaning in the three-term number system from the meaning which it has in the two-term number system. In the two-term number system plural means 'more than one'. In the three-term number system it means 'more than two'.

In order to fully understand the meaning of something, we need to know what it does not mean as well as what it does mean. To take an example from the level of lexis, the lexical item *animal* has some meaning even if it occurs on its own out of any particular context. But we do not know exactly what it means until we know whether it means 'not vegetable or mineral' or 'not human' or 'not bird or reptile or fish'.

By naming a meaning and by assigning it to a system, where it is mutually exclusive with other named meanings, we are able to show both something of what it does include and also what it does not include; what it does not include, that is, of the area of meaning which the terms in the system have in common.

The fact that a system is finite means that a boundary is given to the area of meaning that the terms have in common. All the meanings which form part of the common area are included in the system and are thus inside the boundary. All the meanings which do not form part of the common area are excluded from the system and are thus outside the boundary.

Because a system is finite, we are able to indicate with precision all the meanings which belong to the same area as a given term and all the meanings from that area which the given term excludes. We are also able to indicate, at any rate by implication, the meanings which the given term excludes by reason of their being outside its area of meaning altogether.

Taken together then, the mutually exclusive and finite properties of systems enable us to show, for a given meaning, its relations (or lack of them) with all the other meanings conveyed by the grammar of a language.

It is because a system refers to an area of meaning with a fixed boundary that the meaning of each term in the system depends on the meaning of all the other terms.

The proverbial financial cake will serve as an analogy here. It is a well-known fact that if a certain sum of money is allotted for the use of a certain number of people, one user can enlarge his share of the money only at the expense of the other users. If another person is added to the list of users, the original shares will decrease in value. If someone is removed from the list, the original shares will increase in value.

In a system a certain area of meaning is allotted to a certain number of terms. If one term takes a larger or smaller slice of the meaning, the slices of the other terms vary accordingly. If a new term is added to the system, the slices of the terms already in the system will decrease. As was shown earlier, the plural term in the system of number loses some of its share of the area of meaning if a dual term is added to the system. If a term is removed from the system, the slices of the remaining terms will increase.

8.3　THE ENTRY CONDITIONS FOR SYSTEMS

The point has been stressed that the terms in a system belong to a common area of meaning. A much more precise distinction can be made between things which differ against a common background than between things which are different and which have nothing at all in common. Negative and plural are different, but the difference between them cannot be so sharply defined as the difference between negative and positive, or the difference between singular and plural, which differ within a common framework. Things which differ within a common framework not only differ from each other; they contrast with each other (as indicated in Chapter 4). The terms in a system contrast with each other.

As well as having a common area of meaning, the terms in a system must have a common grammatical environment. Not only must the terms contrast with each other in a common framework of meaning; they must be seen to contrast with each other in a common framework provided by the more surface aspects of grammar.

For each system there is a particular set of circumstances in which the terms of the system, all the terms of the system, are available as choices. This particular set of circumstances must apply before it is possible to make a choice between the terms of the system. Once the particular set of circumstances does apply then it is not only possible to make a choice between the terms of the system, it is in fact obligatory. These circumstances are known as the *entry conditions* for the system.

The first stage in specifying the entry conditions of a system is to state the rank of unit to which the system is applicable.

Each system is applicable to a particular rank of unit. Whenever a new member of that particular rank of unit occurs, a new choice from the system is possible, is not only possible in fact but obligatory. If there is no new member of that particular rank of unit, then no new choice from the system is possible.

For instance, in English the system of mood is applicable to the clause. Whenever a new clause occurs, a new choice from the system of mood is made. Any stretch of language which is not a clause is unable to make a choice from the mood system. In the sentence

Ex. 8.1 *Shut the window or the house will be freezing by the evening*

the clause *Shut the window* has chosen the imperative term from the system. The clause *or the house will be freezing by the evening* is a new clause quite separate from the earlier one and it has therefore made a new and quite separate choice from the system of mood. This second clause has in fact chosen the declarative term. Stretches of language such as *the window* and *by the evening* cannot make choices from the mood system as they are not clauses.

Sometimes a system is applicable to all the members of a unit. In this case it is not necessary to make further specification of the system's entry conditions. Sometimes however a system is applicable only to the members of a unit which are playing a particular part in the structure of a higher unit. In this case it is necessary to specify the grammatical structural environment as well as the rank of unit.

The statement that in English the system of mood is applicable to the clause needs to be qualified. The system is applicable only to clauses which are acting as the α elements of sentences. In the sentence

Ex. 8.2 *Shut the window before you go out or the house will be freezing when we come home*

the two α clauses have chosen respectively the imperative and the declarative, but the two β clauses *before you go out* and *when we come home* have made no choice from the system of mood.

As well as having entry conditions provided for them by unit and structure, systems often provide entry conditions for each other. In many cases it is possible to make a choice from a system only if certain other choices from other systems have been made.

For instance in English it is only possible to make a choice from the system of mood if finite has been chosen in preference to non-finite from the system of finiteness. In the clauses

Ex. 8.3 *Theodore cut me this morning at the supermarket*

Ex. 8.4 *Have you seen Peter anywhere?*

Ex. 8.5 *Close the doors, please*

the term finite has been chosen by the verbal groups and therefore all three clauses have been able to select a term from the mood system, their choices being declarative, interrogative and imperative respectively. However in the clauses

Ex. 8.6 *Turning to the next point*

Ex. 8.7 *To finish the task*

Ex. 8.8 *When completed*

the verbal groups have chosen the term non-finite and therefore the clauses have not been able to choose from the system of mood.

To summarize what has been said in this chapter so far: the terms in a system are meanings; they are meanings between which the grammar of a language makes it possible to choose; they contrast with each other within the framework of a common area of meaning and they contrast with each other within the framework of a common grammatical environment; the mutually exclusive characteristic of a system enables a boundary to be set for the meaning of each term; the finite characteristic of a system enables a boundary to be set for the common area of meaning. By arranging meanings in systems we are able to pinpoint more precisely each particular meaning and we are able to show relationships between meanings within the semantic structure of a language.

8.4 SOME IMPORTANT SYSTEMS OF ENGLISH

8.4.1 *Transitivity Systems*

When we speak or write about anything, usually what we are speaking or writing about will include some kind of *process*.

In the examples

> Ex. 8.9   *John kicked the ball by accident*
> Ex. 8.10   *Theodore saw Mary on Tuesday*
> Ex. 8.11   *Beauty is only skin deep*

the processes of 'kicking', 'seeing' and 'being' are referred to.

Usually there will be *participants* in the process; somebody or something will be involved in the process. In Ex. 8.9 'John' and 'the ball' are involved in the process of 'kicking'. In Ex. 8.10 'Theodore' and 'Mary' are involved in the process of 'seeing'.

Often there will be *circumstances* attendant on the process; the process will have happened at some special time or in some special place or for some special reason. In Ex. 8.9 the 'kicking' happened 'by accident'. In Ex. 8.10 the 'seeing' happened 'on Tuesday'.

There are different types of process. For instance, there are physical processes such as 'kicking', mental processes such as 'seeing' and qualitative processes such as 'being'.

There are also different types of participant. For instance, a participant can be a person such as 'John', or an object such as 'the ball', or an abstraction such as 'beauty'.

Similarly there are different types of circumstance. For instance, a circumstance can be a circumstance of reason such as 'by accident' or a circumstance of time such as 'on Tuesday'.

Not only can participants and circumstances themselves be of different types; they can play different *roles* in a process. In each of the examples

> Ex. 8.10   *Theodore saw Mary on Tuesday*
> Ex. 8.12   *Mary saw Theodore on Tuesday*

the participants are persons. The examples are alike in the type of their participants. But the examples are different in that the participants have switched roles. In Ex. 8.10 'Theodore' is 'the see-er' and 'Mary' is 'the seen', while in Ex. 8.12 the reverse is true.

Processes can have different numbers of participants and circumstances associated with them. The processes of Ex. 8.9 and Ex. 8.10 each have two participants associated with them. The process of

Ex. 8.13   *John ran fast*

has only one.

In English grammar we make choices between different types of process, between different types of participant, between different types of circumstance, between different roles for participants and circumstances, between different numbers of participants and circumstances, between different ways of combining processes, participants and circumstances. These choices are known collectively as the *transitivity* choices.

The clause is the rank of unit which acts as the entry condition for the transitivity choices. Each clause chooses a particular combination of type of process, types of participant and circumstance, numbers of participants and circumstances, participant and circumstance roles.

There is no room in an introductory book of this kind for a comprehensive account of the transitivity systems. The following paragraphs will consider just a few of the choices available under this heading.

As has already been implied, there is a choice between three main types of process: a physical or *material process*; a *mental* process; and what is usually called a *relational* process. Thus we have a system containing three terms:

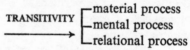

The clauses

Ex. 8.9   *John kicked the ball by accident*
Ex. 8.14   *Peter swam to the island*
Ex. 8.15   *A stream flows through that part of the valley*

have all chosen the term material process.

The clauses

Ex. 8.10   *Theodore saw Mary on Tuesday*
Ex. 8.16   *Children like jelly*
Ex. 8.17   *The vicar said that yesterday*

have all chosen the term mental process.

The clauses

Ex. 8.11   *Beauty is only skin deep*
Ex. 8.18   *Theodore is the vicar's son*
Ex. 8.19   *The family are in the garden*

have all chosen the term relational process.

Material processes can be subdivided. A clause which has chosen the term material process also makes a further choice involving a finer distinction in meaning. Material processes can be either *action* processes, or *event* processes. An action process is the type of material process which is usually performed by an animate being; that is, it is the type of material process which usually has an *animate* participant in the role of *actor*. An event process is the type of material process which is usually performed by an inanimate being; that is, it is the type of material process which usually has an *inanimate* participant in the role of actor. Here we have a system with two terms:

$$\text{material process} \longrightarrow \begin{cases} \text{action process} \\ \text{event process} \end{cases}$$

The clauses

Ex. 8.9   *John kicked the ball by accident*
Ex. 8.14   *Peter swam to the island*

have both chosen the term action process.

The clauses

Ex. 8.15   *A stream flows through that part of the valley*
Ex. 8.20   *The car backfired noisily*

have both chosen the term event process.

In the case of event processes, there is no question of their having been brought about intentionally since inanimate participants do not possess free wills. However action processes may be either intentional or unintentional. For clauses which have chosen the term action process, there is a further choice between *intention* process, a process which the participant in the role of actor performs voluntarily, and *supervention* process, a process which just happens. Again we have a system with two terms:

$$\text{action process} \longrightarrow \begin{cases} \text{intention process} \\ \text{supervention process} \end{cases}$$

The clauses

Ex. 8.14 *Peter swam to the island*
Ex. 8.21 *Tiddles chased a mouse*

have chosen the term intention process.
The clauses

Ex. 8.22 *John tripped over a stone*
Ex. 8.23 *Aunt Jemima dropped the teapot*

have chosen the term supervention process.

Similarly mental processes can be subdivided. Mental processes can be either *internalized* mental processes, such as 'seeing', 'hearing' or 'thinking', or *externalized* mental processes, such as 'saying'.

$$\text{mental process} \longrightarrow \begin{cases} \text{internalized process} \\ \text{externalized process} \end{cases}$$

The clauses

Ex. 8.10 *Theodore saw Mary on Tuesday*
Ex. 8.16 *Children like jelly*
Ex. 8.24 *John considered the matter gravely*

have chosen the term internalized process.
The clauses

Ex. 8.17 *The vicar said that yesterday*
Ex. 8.25 *The curate announced the next hymn*

have chosen the term externalized process.

Internalized mental processes can be further subdivided. Internalized mental processes can be *perception* processes, such as 'seeing' or 'hearing', *reaction* processes, such as 'liking' or 'hating', or *cognition* processes, such as 'thinking'.

$$\text{internalized process} \longrightarrow \begin{cases} \text{perception process} \\ \text{reaction process} \\ \text{cognition process} \end{cases}$$

The clauses

Ex. 8.10 *Theodore saw Mary on Tuesday*
Ex. 8.26 *The crowd listened intently*

have chosen the term perception process.

The clauses

Ex. 8.16 *Children like jelly*
Ex. 8.27 *Caesar hated lean men*

have chosen the term reaction process.
The clauses

Ex. 8.24 *John considered the matter gravely*
Ex. 8.28 *Theodore thought the explanation unlikely*

have chosen the term cognition process.

8.4.2 Voice Systems

Closely associated with the transitivity systems are the *voice* systems.

Given that a particular option has been chosen from a transitivity system, often further choices are possible with respect to the ways in which the option may be represented in the structure of a stretch of language.

Sometimes there is a choice as to whether to represent something in the surface structure at all, whether to actualize something or to leave it inherent; whether, that is, to make something explicit or to leave it implicit.

For instance, given that one is talking about a situation involving a process, one can choose either to be explicit about the process or merely to imply it. In the following conversation three processes are implied:

Ex. 8.29 A *Black coffee?*
       B *White, please.*

In the following conversation these three processes (or something like them) are made explicit:

Ex. 8.30 A *Would you like black coffee?*
       B *I should prefer white, if you don't mind.*

We have here a system (sometimes called the system of *majority*) consisting of two terms

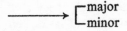

The term *major* is used to refer to the making of a process explicit. The term *minor* is used to refer to the leaving of a process implicit.

When a process has been made explicit, this will show in the surface structure of a clause since the clause will contain a predicator. When a process has been left implicit, the structure of the clause will not contain a predicator. The structures of the clauses *Would you like black coffee?*, *I should prefer white* and *if you don't mind* all contain predicators. The structures of the clauses *Black coffee?*, *White* and *please* do not contain predicators.

When something *is* to be represented in the surface structure of a stretch of language, there is sometimes a choice of elements by which it can be represented.

For instance a participant in the role of actor can be represented either by the subject of a clause or by an adjunct. In

Ex. 8.31 *John kicked the ball*

the participant in the role of actor is represented by the subject of the clause. In

Ex. 8.32 *The ball was kicked by John*

the participant in the role of actor is represented by an adjunct.

A participant in the role of goal (the *goal* of a process is the person or thing acted upon by the process) can be represented either by the complement of a clause or by the subject. In Ex. 8.31 the participant in the role of goal, the 'ball', is represented by the complement. In Ex. 8.32 this participant in the role of goal is represented by the subject.

Here we have a system (the system which is traditionally called *voice*)[1] with the terms *active* (actor represented by subject, goal represented by complement) and *passive* (actor represented by adjunct, goal represented by subject).

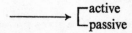

As well as the choices relating to if and where to represent a transitivity option in surface structure, there are choices relating to the usualness of combinations of transitivity options. Given that two options are potentially very likely to occur together, it is still possible to choose not to combine them in an actual stretch of language. Given that two options are potentially very unlikely to occur together, it is still possible to choose to combine them in an actual stretch of language.

For instance, as was indicated in Section 8.4.1, the action type of

---

[1] It should be noted that the term *voice* is used in this book in a much wider sense than that in which it is usually used.

process is usually combined with an animate type of participant in the role of actor while the event type of process is usually combined with an inanimate type of participant in the role of actor. It is, however, possible to combine action type of process with inanimate type of participant and to combine event type of process with animate type of participant. In

Ex. 8.33 *The door waltzed open* (Dorothy L. Sayers, *Clouds o, Witness*)

an action type of process is combined with an inanimate type of participant. In

Ex. 8.34 *Theodore flowed into the room*

an event type of process is combined with an animate type of participant. The implication of Ex. 8.33 would be that the door was being personified. The implication of Ex. 8.34 would be that Theodore, although human, had some of the qualities of a particular kind of inanimate participant.

There is a choice here between a *typical* combination of transitivity options and an *untypical* combination.

$$\longrightarrow \begin{bmatrix} \text{typical} \\ \text{untypical} \end{bmatrix}$$

The examples given in Section 8.4.1 (Ex. 8.9, Ex. 8.14, Ex. 8.15 and Ex. 8.20) have chosen typical. The examples given above (Ex. 8.33 and Ex. 8.34) have chosen untypical.

> There is a sense in which the choice between active and passive is also a typical/untypical kind of choice since it is more usual for a participant in the role of actor to be represented by the subject and a participant in the role of goal to be represented by the complement than it is for a participant in the role of actor to be represented by an adjunct and a participant in the role of goal to be represented by the subject.

These systems relating to the actualization and bringing to the surface of the transitivity options are known collectively as the *voice* systems. As might be expected from the close relationship between these systems and the transitivity systems, the clause is again the rank of unit which acts as an entry condition.

There is no more room in a book of this kind for a comprehensive account of the voice systems than there was for a comprehensive account of the transitivity systems. Again the discussion must be restricted to just a few of the possible choices.

Before more of the voice systems can be considered it is necessary to introduce a few more of the transitivity systems. The transitivity systems presented in Section 8.4.1 were, in the main, systems relating to choices between types of process, although matters relating to types of participant and participant role were occasionally relevant. In this section we shall be mainly concerned with transitivity systems relating to choices between different numbers of participants. Matters relating to participant roles will also be relevant.

Different types of process have different potentialities for combining with particular numbers of participants and particular participant roles. For instance, the options relating to the number of participants and participant roles which are available to material processes are different from those available to mental processes which are in turn different from those available to relational processes. There is room in this section only to consider some of the number of participants choices and participant role choices available to material processes.

Attention should be drawn to the fact that when we arrange terms in systems, as in Section 8.4.1, we are doing so not only on the basis of their meanings, but also on the basis of their potentialities for combining with other options.

Some material processes combine fairly freely with differing numbers of participants, while other material processes are associated with a relatively fixed number of participants. Processes such as 'opening', 'breaking', 'warming', occur about as frequently with one participant as they do with two participants. Processes such as 'hitting', 'throwing', 'kicking' almost always occur with two participants. Clauses which have chosen the term material process make a choice between *unrestricted* process (the type of process which combines equally well with either one or two participants) and *restricted* process (the type of process which is associated with a relatively fixed number of participants).

$$\text{material process} \longrightarrow \begin{cases} \text{unrestricted process} \\ \text{restricted process} \end{cases}$$

The clauses

Ex. 8.35 *John opened the door*
Ex. 8.36 *The door opened*
Ex. 8.37 *Aunt Jemima broke the teapot*
Ex. 8.38 *The teapot broke*
Ex. 8.39 *Mary warmed the milk*
Ex. 8.40 *The milk warmed gradually*

have all chosen the term unrestricted process.

The clauses

Ex. 8.41 *The car hit the kerb*
Ex. 8.42 *The wicket-keeper threw the ball in the air*
Ex. 8.43 *Billy has just kicked his sister*

have all chosen the term restricted process.

All the examples of restricted processes given so far have been processes for which the 'relatively fixed number of participants' is two. There are also restricted processes for which the 'relatively fixed number of participants' is one. The former of these kinds of restricted process almost always occurs with both actor and goal. The latter almost always occurs with only actor. Restricted processes choose between being *middle* (associated with actor only) and *non-middle* (associated with both actor and goal).

$$\text{restricted process} \longrightarrow \begin{bmatrix} \text{middle} \\ \text{non-middle} \end{bmatrix}$$

Exs. 8.41, 8.42, and 8.43 are examples of clauses which have chosen non-middle.

Examples of clauses which have chosen middle are:

Ex. 8.44 *Peter ran energetically*
Ex. 8.45 *Theodore walked slowly*
Ex. 8.46 *Mary danced round the room*
Ex. 8.47 *Aunt Jemima will live for a long time yet.*

Processes which are middle are often to do with physical exercise such as 'running', 'walking', 'dancing' or physical existence such as 'living' and 'dying'.

We can distinguish then between processes for which we do not have any particular expectancy as regards number of participants (unrestricted processes) and processes which we expect to occur with a particular number of participants (restricted processes). We can subdivide restricted processes into those which we expect to occur with one participant (middle) and those which we expect to occur with two (non-middle).

We can also subdivide unrestricted processes. When unrestricted processes occur with two participants there is usually an implication of 'causation' in their meaning. Ex. 8.35, *John opened the door* can be paraphrased as 'John caused the door to open'. Ex. 8.37 *Aunt Jemima broke the teapot* can be paraphrased as 'Aunt Jemima caused the teapot to break'. Ex. 8.39 *Mary warmed the milk* can be paraphrased as 'Mary caused the milk to warm'. When unrestricted processes occur with only one participant the 'causation' part of the meaning is absent. Clauses which have chosen the term unrestricted process choose between *causative* and *non-causative*.

$$\text{unrestricted process} \longrightarrow \begin{bmatrix} \text{causative} \\ \text{non-causative} \end{bmatrix}$$

Exs 8.35, 8.37 and 8.39 are examples of clauses which have chosen causative.

Examples of clauses which have chosen non-causative are:

Ex. 8.36   *The door opened*
Ex. 8.38   *The teapot broke*
Ex. 8.40   *The milk warmed gradually.*

In the clauses which have chosen causative, the apparent actors ('John', 'Aunt Jemima' and 'Mary') are actors of the 'causing', not actors of the clauses' main processes ('opening', 'breaking' and 'warming'). The apparent goals ('the door', 'the teapot' and 'the milk') are the goals of the 'causing'; they are also the actors of the main processes.

In the last few pages we have met three new transitivity systems: unrestricted/restricted, middle/non-middle, causative/non-causative. Let us now consider some of the voice systems associated with them.

It has already been said that non-middle processes are associated with both actor and goal. The goal can either be made explicit or left implicit. A clause which has chosen non-middle can choose between *transitive* (making its goal explicit) and *intransitive* (leaving its goal implicit).

$$\text{non-middle} \longrightarrow \begin{bmatrix} \text{transitive} \\ \text{intransitive} \end{bmatrix}$$

The clauses

Ex. 8.48   *Cover point threw the ball wildly to the wicket-keeper*
Ex. 8.49   *I have been washing the clothes all afternoon*
Ex. 8.50   *Peter hit his opponent hard*

have chosen transitive.

The clauses

Ex. 8.51   *Cover point threw wildly to the wicket-keeper*
Ex. 8.52   *I have been washing all afternoon*
Ex. 8.53   *Peter hit hard*

have chosen intransitive.

It should be emphasized that the transitivity distinction middle/non-middle is a different distinction from the voice distinction transitive/intransitive. The middle/non-middle distinction is based on the number of participants inherent in a process. The transitive/intransitive distinction is based on the number of participants actually represented in the surface structure of a stretch of language (given that there are two inherent participants).

Clauses which have chosen both non-middle and passive can choose between making their actor explicit or leaving it implicit.

$$\text{passive} \longrightarrow \left[\begin{array}{l}\text{actor explicit}\\\text{actor implicit}\end{array}\right.$$

The clauses

Ex. 8.54 *The ball was thrown to the wicket-keeper by cover point*
Ex. 8.55 *The rose-beds have been weeded by the gardener*
Ex. 8.56 *The lamp-post was hit by the car*

have chosen actor explicit.
The clauses

Ex. 8.57 *The ball was thrown to the wicket-keeper*
Ex. 8.58 *The rose-beds have been weeded*
Ex. 8.59 *The lamp-post was hit*

have chosen actor implicit.

It has been shown that the term causative is a subdivision of the term unrestricted process. Restricted processes do not usually combine with the term causative. However the middle kind of restricted process can on occasion combine with causative. When this happens the middle process will have two participants associated with it, not just the one participant which is usually inherent in it. Here we have an example of a voice system based on the choice between a typical or untypical combination of transitivity options.

$$\text{middle} \longrightarrow \left[\begin{array}{l}\text{typical}\\\text{untypical}\end{array}\right.$$

The clauses

Ex. 8.44 *Peter ran energetically*
Ex. 8.45 *Theodore walked slowly*
Ex. 8.46 *Mary danced round the room*

have chosen typical middle.

The clauses

Ex. 8.60 *Her excited daughter danced Mary round the room*
Ex. 8.61 *They ran him out of town*
Ex. 8.62 *John walked the horse up and down*

have chosen untypical middle.

The voice systems, then, are choices between different ways of actualizing and bringing to the surface the transitivity options. As we have seen, they involve choices between explicitness and implicitness, choices between whether or not to represent something by the most usual element of surface structure, choices between usual and unusual combinations of transitivity options.

The reasons why, in a given situation, we choose one rather than another of the terms of a voice system are many and various.

We may, for instance, choose an implicit option in preference to an explicit option because there is no need to be explicit, because it is obvious from the situation or from the surrounding text what we are talking about. This is often the reason for choosing intransitive in preference to transitive. In Ex. 8.51, for example, we can deduce fairly confidently that what cover point threw was a ball, even though we are not told so explicitly. He is unlikely to have thrown anything else.

Sometimes it just does not matter whether a particular participant or circumstance is made clear to our hearers. If this particular participant or circumstance is not central to what we are saying, we can afford to leave it vague. This is often the reason for choosing actor implicit in preference to actor explicit. In these cases it is often the process itself which is important. We assume that someone was responsible for performing the process, but it is quite irrelevant to state who the performer was. The implication of Ex. 8.58, for example, is presumably that what is important is that the rose-beds have been weeded. It does not matter who did the weeding as long as they have been weeded and are no longer in need of attention.

Sometimes vagueness is a positive advantage. In an informal situation one neither needs nor wants to be too precise. Too great explicitness immediately puts a conversation on a formal footing. This is often the reason for choosing minor in preference to major. Ex. 8.29 would be much more natural in an informal situation than Ex. 8.30. Ex. 8.30 would be more appropriate at a very formal coffee party at which hostess and guests do not know each other well and everyone is on their best behaviour.

We usually choose an untypical combination of transitivity options in preference to a typical combination when we want to imply that something (or someone) has a characteristic other than those which we would normally attribute to it. We choose the untypical combination of action process and inanimate actor when we want to personify the inanimate actor. We choose the untypical combination of event process and animate actor when we want to depersonify, or partly depersonify, the animate actor. We choose the untypical combination of middle and causative when we want to imply that the kind of process we normally perform of our own free will is being imposed on someone.

The reasons for choosing an option such as passive in preference to an option such as active are similar to those for choosing some of the theme options, and will be discussed in the next section.

> Recent work by Professor Halliday (Halliday, forthcoming) and by Mr David Evans (in a preliminary draft of a PhD thesis for the University of Nottingham) has shown that a number of the systems discussed in Sections 8.4.1 and 8.4.2 are really clines. However the clines still need to be segmented for the purposes of analysis. (See 2.1.4.)

8.4.3 Theme Systems

We have several times in this book met the distinction between unmarked (usual) and marked (unusual) forms of language. We met it in Chapter 4, in connection with latent patterns, which were explained in terms of an unusual frequency of occurrence contrasting with a usual frequency of occurrence. We met it in Chapter 5, in connection with the order of elements of structure, in connection with the uses of classes of formal items, and in connection with the functions associated with elements of structure. We met it in Section 8.4.2 in connection with combinations of transitivity options and in connection with the representation of particular participant roles by particular elements of structure.

> Some of these kinds of unmarked/marked distinction overlap. The last-mentioned kind of unmarked/marked distinction, exemplified in Section 8.4.2 by the active/passive system, is actually the same unmarked/marked distinction as one of the kinds discussed in Chapter 5 in connection with the functions associated with elements of structure. In Chapter 5 this kind of unmarked/marked distinction was viewed from a structural angle. In the present chapter it has been viewed from a systemic angle. Certain of the other unmarked/marked distinctions discussed in Chapter 5 are the same kind of unmarked/ marked distinction as the kind to be discussed in this section of the present chapter.

The *theme* systems are based on the unmarked/marked distinction. The theme systems are choices between different ways of arranging the basic ingredients of a message in an order of prominence. The basic ingredients which the theme options arrange are precisely those which have been discussed already under the heading of *transitivity*: the processes, participants and circumstances.

> Processes, participants and circumstances are not of course the only basic ingredients of a message. They simply happen to be the ones with which theme is concerned. Nor are the theme systems the only systems concerned with arranging things in order of prominence.

The first place in a clause and the last place in a clause are significant in English for the giving of prominence to something. The first place is significant simply because it is first, because it is the first thing to catch the hearer's or reader's attention. The reason for the significance of the last place will be indicated in Volume II Chapter 4.

Just by putting one of the basic ingredients of a message in first place or last place we give it some prominence. If in so doing we are also putting it in an unusual position, this gives it even greater prominence. If as well as putting it in first or last place and in an unusual position we perform other operations on it, we are giving it greater prominence still. In

Ex. 8.63   *The meeting takes place on Tuesday*

'the meeting' has some prominence since it comes first and 'Tuesday' and some prominence since it comes last. The prominence is very slight however and we scarcely notice it, since both 'the meeting' and 'on Tuesday' are represented in quite usual positions. In

Ex. 8.64   *On Tuesday the meeting takes place*

On Tuesday has been moved to first place, which is a less usual position for it, with the result that 'Tuesday' is given greater prominence. If, as well as moving it to the front, we enclose it in other words whose sole purpose is to single it out, as in

Ex. 8.65   *It's on Tuesday that the meeting takes place*

'Tuesday' is given still greater prominence.

In view of the fact that it is the basic ingredients produced by the transitivity options that the theme options are arranging, it is not surprising to find that the clause is again the rank of unit which provides the entry condition.

Again it must be said that there is no room in the book for a full discussion of the topic. Again a few examples of systems must suffice.

Each clause chooses between *unmarked theme* and *marked theme*. For a material process clause this means that the clause chooses between representing the participant in the role of actor in first place and representing something other than the participant in the role of actor in first place. This distinction shows in the surface structure of a clause, since a clause which has chosen unmarked theme will have the element s in the first place, while a clause which has chosen marked theme will have P, C or A in first place.

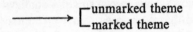

The clauses

Ex. 8.66   *I shall complete this to-morrow or Friday*
Ex. 8.67   *You can find shells on the seashore*
Ex. 8.68   *(And) they ran all the way home*

have chosen unmarked theme.

The clauses

Ex. 8.69   *This I shall complete to-morrow or Friday*
Ex. 8.70   *On the seashore you can find shells*
Ex. 8.71   *(And) run they did all the way home*

have chosen marked theme. In Ex. 8.69 the participant in the role of goal has been given prominence by being represented in first place. In Ex. 8.70 a circumstance has been given prominence by being represented in first place. In Ex. 8.71 the process has been given prominence by being represented in first place.

Since the unmarked theme/marked theme distinction and the active/passive distinction are in some ways alike, it is perhaps worthwhile to compare and contrast them.

Both the marked theme option and the passive option have the effect of representing in the significant first place of a clause something other than the actor, the actor being the participant which is usually represented in first place. Both often also have the effect of representing something unusual in the other significant place, the last place. This is particularly true of the passive, which usually represents either the actor or the process itself in last place.

Although marked theme and passive have these similar effects, they achieve the effects by different means. The marked theme option achieves its effect by shifting a whole element of structure and placing it in an unusual position in the clause. The passive option merely detaches a function from the element of structure usually associated with that function and assigns it to another element of structure. (See Chapter 5.) For the passive option the elements of structure of a clause remain in what is more or less usual order.

It is perhaps because marked theme involves shifting a whole element that it seems more unusual, more marked, than the passive, although both are marked in comparison with their respective partners, unmarked theme and active.

Each clause chooses between *non-predicated theme* and *predicated theme*. A clause which chooses non-predicated theme leaves whatever occurs in first place unadorned by any special singling-out device. A clause which chooses predicated theme encloses whatever occurs in first place in a construction such as *it* + part of the verb *be* + *who/which/that*.

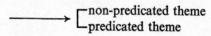

$$\longrightarrow \left[\begin{array}{l}\text{non-predicated theme}\\\text{predicated theme}\end{array}\right.$$

The clauses

Ex. 8.72   *Peter swam the fastest*
Ex. 8.73   *The Tone flows through that valley*
Ex. 8.74   *On Friday I'm going to the cinema*
Ex. 8.75   *On the shore Peter cut his foot*

have chosen non-predicated theme.
The clauses

Ex. 8.76   *It was Peter who swam the fastest*
Ex. 8.77   *It's the Tone that flows through that valley*
Ex. 8.78   *It's on Friday that I'm going to the cinema*
Ex. 8.79   *It was on the shore that Peter cut his foot*

have chosen predicated theme.

Each clause chooses between *non-preposed theme* and *preposed theme*. A clause which has chosen non-preposed theme makes use only of regular places in clause structure to give prominence to ingredients. A clause which has chosen preposed theme makes use of an extra place before the clause structure proper begins. In this case the ingredient to be given prominence is represented twice, once in the extra place in front of the clause and once in its normal position in the clause structure. The second representation is usually by means of a substitute form such as a pronoun.

$$\longrightarrow \left[\begin{array}{l}\text{non-preposed theme}\\\text{preposed theme}\end{array}\right.$$

The clauses

Ex. 8.80   *Snowdon is a mountain to be respected*
Ex. 8.81   *We saw a flower festival in Amsterdam*
Ex. 8.82   *Stoke Pero Church had seven pages of visitors during October*

have chosen non-preposed theme.

The clauses

Ex. 8.83   *Snowdon, that's a mountain to be respected*
Ex. 8.84   *Amsterdam, we saw a flower festival there*
Ex. 8.85   *Stoke Pero Church, they had seven pages of visitors during October*

have chosen preposed theme.

Preposed theme is more common in conversational spoken English than in other varieties of English. It is not confined to the conversational register, however, as can be seen from the prayer which follows the Prayer of Consecration in the Series Two version of the Anglican Communion Service (based on I Corinthians 10 : 16).

There are various reasons for giving prominence to a particular ingredient.

It may be simply that the ingredient is particularly important, particularly worth emphasizing.

It may be that the ingredient is a starting point for what is to come, a topic about which the other ingredients are providing a comment. For instance, a clause which has chosen preposed theme is almost like a headline or title followed by a news item.

It may be that the ingredient is providing a link with what has gone before, referring back to something which has already been mentioned. This would appear to be the reason for giving prominence to *This* in Ex. 8.69.

It may, however, be for the opposite reason, that the ingredient is the one of the ingredients which is least deducible from what has gone before, that it is the new bit of information. Ex. 8.78 could be spoken in such a way as to suggest that the hearer already knows that I am going to the cinema. What he does not know is which day I am going.

The ingredient may be in direct contrast with something which has gone before. The hearer of Ex. 8.78 might previously have indicated that he thought I was going to the cinema on Thursday. Ex. 8.78 might be an attempt to correct him.

It may be for a combination of these reasons.

It is impossible without a full discussion of all the theme systems to give a full account of the reasons for choosing particular options from the systems. The systems interact and often it is only possible to interpret the choice of an option from one theme system in the light of the options which have been chosen from other theme systems.

8.4.4 *Mood Systems*

So far in Section 8.4 we have considered systems relating to the basic ingredients of a message; we have considered systems relating to the actualization and bringing to the surface of these basic ingredients; and we have considered systems relating to the arrangement in order of prominence of these basic ingredients.

In Section 8.4.4 we shall not be concerned so much with the basic message as with the speaker and hearer (or writer and reader) of the message and the roles which they adopt in relation to each other.

The *mood* systems are choices between different roles which a speaker can select for himself and for his hearer.

As was shown earlier in the chapter, the clause is again the rank of unit which provides the entry condition, but whereas all clauses choose from transitivity, voice and theme systems, only clauses acting as α elements choose from the mood systems. It was also shown earlier in the chapter that the choice of finite in preference to non-finite was a necessary condition for entry to a mood system.

Let us now consider some of the mood systems.

Each α clause chooses between *indicative* and *imperative*. The speaker of a clause which has chosen imperative has selected for himself the role of controller and for his hearer the role of controlled. The speaker expects from the hearer more than a purely verbal response. He expects some form of action. The speaker of a clause which has chosen indicative has not selected the roles of controller and controlled for himself and his hearer. If he is expecting any response from his hearer, it is purely verbal response that he expects.

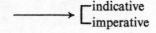

The clauses

Ex. 8.86   *Has John closed the door?*
Ex. 8.87   *Small boys are naturally dirty*
Ex. 8.88   *Well-trained dogs keep to heel*

have chosen indicative.

The clauses

Ex. 8.89   *Close the door, Theodore*
Ex. 8.90   *Wash behind your ears*
Ex. 8.91   *Keep to heel*

have chosen imperative.

A clause which has chosen indicative makes a further choice between *declarative* and *interrogative*. The speaker of a clause which has chosen declarative has selected for himself the role of informant and for his hearer the role of informed. The speaker of a clause which has chosen interrogative has selected for himself the role of informed and for his hearer the role of informant. The speaker of a clause which has chosen interrogative is expecting a verbal response from his hearer. The speaker of a clause which has chosen declarative is not necessarily expecting an overt response.

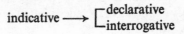

$$\text{indicative} \longrightarrow \begin{cases} \text{declarative} \\ \text{interrogative} \end{cases}$$

The clauses

Ex. 8.92   *The post has come*
Ex. 8.93   *Here is some string*
Ex. 8.94   *John is in London*

have chosen declarative.

The clauses

Ex. 8.95   *Has the post come?*
Ex. 8.96   *Have you any string?*
Ex. 8.97   *Where is John?*

have chosen interrogative.

A clause which has chosen interrogative makes a further choice between *closed interrogative* and *open interrogative*. The speaker of a clause which has chosen closed interrogative expects his hearer to make one of a very limited number of responses; in effect he expects him to say either yes or no. The speaker of a clause which has chosen open interrogative has more open-ended expectations as regards his hearer's response.

$$\text{interrogative} \longrightarrow \begin{cases} \text{closed interrogative} \\ \text{open interrogative} \end{cases}$$

The clauses

Ex. 8.98   *Do you like coffee?*
Ex. 8.99   *Have you a car?*
Ex. 8.100 *Is the meeting tomorrow?*

have chosen closed interrogative.
The clauses

Ex. 8.101 *What is your favourite drink?*
Ex. 8.102 *Where is your car?*
Ex. 8.103 *When is the meeting?*

have chosen open interrogative.

A clause which has chosen imperative makes a further choice between *exclusive imperative* and *inclusive imperative*. The speaker of a clause which has chosen exclusive imperative excludes himself from the performers of the action he is advocating. The speaker of a clause which has chosen inclusive imperative includes himself among the performers of the action he is advocating.

$$\text{imperative} \longrightarrow \begin{bmatrix} \text{exclusive imperative} \\ \text{inclusive imperative} \end{bmatrix}$$

The examples of imperatives given so far, Exs 8.89, 8.90 and 8.91 are all examples of exclusive imperatives.
Examples of inclusive imperatives are

Ex. 8.104 *Let's go to the cinema*
Ex. 8.105 *Let us now praise famous men*
Ex. 8.106 *Let us consider the matter.*

8.4.5   *Modality Systems*

The *modality* systems, like the mood systems, are concerned with the speaker (or writer) of a message. The modality systems however are not concerned with the speaker in relation to his hearer so much as with the speaker's attitude towards his message. They are concerned with the speaker's assessment of the probability of the truth of his message.

The clause is again the rank of unit which provides the entry condition, but again not all clauses can choose from the modality systems. Only clauses which have chosen indicative and declarative from the mood systems can make choices from the modality systems.

Clauses which have chosen interrogative do make some choices from modality systems but the range of options open to them is not the same as the range open to declarative clauses.

A declarative clause chooses between *modality neutral* and *modality assessed*. A clause which has chosen modality neutral makes no reference to the certainty or otherwise of its basic message. In such a case we assume that the speaker considers the truth of his message to be certain. A clause which has chosen modality assessed makes some reference to the certainty or otherwise of its basic message. In this case the speaker may be far from certain, moderately certain, almost certain of the truth of his message. (The speaker of a clause which has chosen modality assessed never seems to be absolutely certain of the truth of his message. It is said that to mention honour is to question it. It almost seems as if the same is true of the mention of certainty.)

$$\text{declarative} \longrightarrow \begin{bmatrix} \text{modality neutral} \\ \text{modality assessed} \end{bmatrix}$$

The clauses

Ex. 8.107 *It is raining*
Ex. 8.108 *She will come tomorrow*
Ex. 8.109 *That's John*

have chosen modality neutral.
The clauses

Ex. 8.110 *It must be raining*
Ex. 8.111 *She will probably come to-morrow*
Ex. 8.112 *That may be John*

have chosen modality assessed.
A clause which has chosen modality assessed makes a further choice between *possible, probable* and *almost certain*.

$$\text{modality assessed} \longrightarrow \begin{bmatrix} \text{possible} \\ \text{probable} \\ \text{almost certain} \end{bmatrix}$$

The clauses

Ex. 8.112 *That may be John*
Ex. 8.113 *I may possibly be late*
Ex. 8.114 *Perhaps the train has gone*

have chosen possible.

The clauses

Ex. 8.115   *That's probably John*
Ex. 8.116   *He will probably be here by now*
Ex. 8.117   *The train has probably gone*

have chosen probable.

The clauses

Ex. 8.110   *It must be raining*
Ex. 8.118   *He must certainly be here by now*
Ex. 8.119   *The train must have gone*

have chosen almost certain.

Again it must be stressed that the account given here is far from being a complete coverage of the topic.

8.4.6   *Episode Linkage Systems*

In this section we are returning to a consideration of the basic message.

Usually when we speak or write we are not concerned with just one episode in isolation; we are not concerned, that is, with just one process and its associated participants and circumstances. We are concerned with a number of episodes, with a number of processes and their associated participants and circumstances. These episodes, these processes with their participants and circumstances, are usually related in some way.

In

Ex. 8.120   *Since the availability of the pitch is uncertain the committee have postponed the match against the next village*

there are two processes: a process of 'being' in the first part and a process of 'postponing' in the second part. Each process has participants associated with it. Each process together with its participants is an episode. The two episodes are related, as is shown by the word *since*.

Episode linkage systems are choices between different kinds of relationship which can exist between episodes. The rank of unit which acts as the entry condition is the complex clause (or sentence).

The episode linkage systems which have the complex clause as an entry condition are not the only systems concerned with relationships between episodes. We could relate the two episodes of Ex. 8.120

by means of options from systems which have other ranks of unit as entry conditions. We could say

Ex. 8.121 *The availability of the pitch is uncertain. For this reason the committee have postponed the match against the next village.*

Or we could say

Ex. 8.122 *The uncertainty about the availability of the pitch has resulted in the postponement by the committee of the match against the next village.*

In Ex. 8.121 the linkage is at the rank of paragraph. In Ex. 8.122 the linkage is at the rank of simplex (as opposed to complex) clause.

A complex clause chooses between *episodes parallel, episodes tangential* and *episodes related*. The episodes of a complex clause which has chosen episodes parallel are, as the name of the term suggests, in some way parallel to each other. Often the episodes have the same type of process (if not exactly the same process) and the same type of participant (if not exactly the same participant). The episodes of a complex clause which has chosen episodes tangential share a participant or share a circumstance but in other ways are not much alike. Whereas parallel episodes are alike in more than one of their basic ingredients, tangential episodes are connected through only one ingredient. The episodes of a complex clause which has chosen episodes related are much more closely related than either episodes which simply happen to be alike or episodes which simply happen to share an ingredient. For instance related episodes may be temporally related. One episode may not take place until the other has been completed. Or they may be causally related. The occurrence of one of the episodes may be dependent on the occurrence of the other.

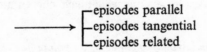

The complex clauses

Ex. 8.123 *Peter bought a Ford, John bought a Morris and Theodore purchased a Bentley*
Ex. 8.124 *The baby is blue-eyed and has fair hair*
Ex. 8.125 *The trees swayed and the washing billowed on the line*

have chosen episodes parallel.

The complex clauses

Ex. 8.126　*Mrs Smith, who is apparently John's mother, rang me up the other day*

Ex. 8.127　*I saw Mary at the Senate House, where my meeting was taking place*

Ex. 8.128　*Tiddles, who belongs to Aunt Jemima, is a tabby*

have chosen episodes tangential.

The complex clauses

Ex. 8.120　*Since the availability of the pitch is uncertain, the committee have postponed the match against the next village*

Ex. 8.129　*When we have completed Stage One of the project, we shall begin on Stage Two*

Ex. 8.130　*The lamb went wherever Mary went*

have chosen episodes related.

Complex clauses which have chosen episodes parallel make a further choice between *co-existent* and *mutually exclusive* episodes. A complex clause which has chosen co-existent makes no suggestion that there is any incompatibility between its episodes. There is no reason to believe that, given that one of the episodes has occurred, it is unlikely that the other episode will have occurred also. A complex clause which has chosen mutually exclusive suggests that there is some incompatibility between its episodes, that it is unlikely that both episodes would occur.

$$\text{episodes parallel} \longrightarrow \begin{cases} \text{co-existent episodes} \\ \text{mutually exclusive episodes} \end{cases}$$

The examples of parallel episodes given above, Exs 8.123, 8.124 and 8.125, are all examples of co-existent episodes.

Examples of complex clauses which have chosen mutually exclusive episodes are:

Ex. 8.131　*Would you like coffee or do you prefer tea?*

Ex. 8.132　*Speak now or forever hold your peace*

Ex. 8.133　*He either fell or was pushed.*

Complex clauses which have chosen mutually exclusive episodes make a further choice between *expectation and fact concord* and *expectation and fact discord*. A complex clause which has chosen expectation and fact concord gives no indication that in actual fact its episodes will turn out to be less incompatible than they were expected to be. A complex clause which has chosen expectation and fact discord indicates that although its episodes might have been expected to be incompatible, they in fact turned out to be co-existent.

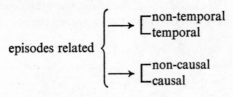

$$\text{mutually exclusive episodes} \longrightarrow \begin{cases} \text{expectation and fact concord} \\ \text{expectation and fact discord} \end{cases}$$

The examples of mutually exclusive episodes given above, Exs 8.131, 8.132 and 8.133, are all examples of expectation and fact concord.

Examples of complex clauses which have chosen expectation and fact discord are:

Ex. 8.134   *She preferred coffee but drank tea*
Ex. 8.135   *He was pushed but did not fall*
Ex. 8.136   *They were hungry but would not eat.*

Complex clauses which have chosen episodes related make a number of further choices. To give just two instances, they choose between *non-temporal* relation and *temporal* relation and between *non-causal* relation and *causal* relation.

$$\text{episodes related} \begin{cases} \longrightarrow \begin{cases} \text{non-temporal} \\ \text{temporal} \end{cases} \\ \\ \longrightarrow \begin{cases} \text{non-causal} \\ \text{causal} \end{cases} \end{cases}$$

The complex clauses

Ex. 8.137   *You'll find the stone where the road forks*
Ex. 8.138   *Mary walks as gracefully as Susan dances*

have chosen non-temporal and non-causal.

The complex clauses

Ex. 8.139   *Just as the play was starting, the Smiths took their seats*
Ex. 8.140   *There was a phone-call while you were at the meeting*

have chosen temporal and non-causal.

The complex clauses

Ex. 8.120   *Since the availability of the pitch is uncertain, the committee have postponed the match against the next village*
Ex. 8.141   *He pitied her because she was so helpless*

have chosen non-temporal and causal.

The complex clauses

Ex. 8.142   *When he is present, it is virtually impossible to talk to you*
Ex. 8.143   *While it is raining the clothes will not dry*

have chosen causal and temporal.

Just as the transitivity systems have associated systems which are choices between different ways of bringing their options to the surface, so too do the episode linkage systems.

As in the case of the transitivity systems, there is a choice between different degrees of explicitness. The following complex clauses have all chosen episodes related and causal relation from the episode linkage systems. They vary, however, in the degree of explicitness with which the causal relation is represented in the surface structure.

Ex. 8.120   *Since the availability of the pitch is uncertain, the committee have postponed the match against the next village*
Ex. 8.144   *The availability of the pitch being uncertain, the committee
            have postponed the match against the next village*
Ex. 8.145   *The availability of the pitch is uncertain and the committee
            have postponed the match against the next village*

Ex. 8.120 has chosen *relation explicit*. The fact that the structure includes a β element shows that there is a relation of dependency between the episodes. The word *since* makes it explicit that this is a causal relation. Ex. 8.144 has chosen *relation partially explicit*. The fact that the structure includes a β element shows that there is a relation of dependency between the episodes. But there is nothing in the surface structure to make explicit what the relation is. Ex. 8.145 has chosen *relation inexplicit*. The structure consists of two α elements. The *and* acknowledges that there is some connection between the episodes but there is nothing to indicate a relation of dependency, let alone to make explicit what that relation is. A causal relation complex clause which has chosen relation inexplicit looks superficially like a complex clause which has chosen episodes parallel.

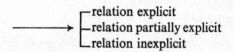

As in the case of the transitivity systems, there is sometimes a choice as to which element of structure shall represent which participant role. In Ex. 8.120 the episode 'the availability of the pitch is uncertain' is in the role of cause while the episode 'the committee have postponed the match against the next village' is in the role of effect. In Ex. 8.120 the episode in the role of cause is represented by the β element while the episode in the role of effect is represented by the α element.

In

Ex. 8.146 *The availability of the pitch is uncertain with the result that the committee have postponed the match against the next village*

the episode in the role of cause is represented by the α element while the episode in the role of effect is represented by the β element.

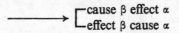

Just as the transitivity systems have associated systems which are choices between different ways of arranging ingredients in order of prominence, so too do the episode linkage systems.

In Ex. 8.120 the β element occurs in first position.

In

Ex. 8.147 *The committee have postponed the match against the next village since the availability of the pitch is uncertain*

the α element is in first position.

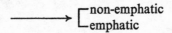

It should be noted that altering the order of the elements does not affect the question of which role is represented by which element.

Sometimes there is a choice as to whether to add an extra word or words in the surface structure in order to emphasize a particular relation.

$$\longrightarrow \begin{bmatrix} \text{non-emphatic} \\ \text{emphatic} \end{bmatrix}$$

The complex clauses

Ex. 8.132 *Speak now or forever hold your peace*
Ex. 8.148 *He fell or was pushed*

have chosen non-emphatic.

The complex clauses

Ex. 8.149 *Either speak now or forever hold your peace*
Ex. 8.133 *He either fell or was pushed*

have chosen emphatic.

The reasons for choosing one rather than another of the options of the last four systems mentioned are similar to those discussed in relation to voice and theme.

It must again be stressed that it is impossible to give an adequate account of a topic of this complexity in just a few pages. The aim of this section, as of the other sections of the chapter, has been to give an indication of the range of kinds of system rather than to explore a particular area of the grammar in detail.

Since the subject matter of Chapter 8 and the subject matter of Chapter 9 are so closely related, they will be discussed together in the Discussion section at the end of Chapter 9.

9
Grammar: Delicacy

9.1 DELICACY

In Section 8.4.1 we considered systems relating to types of process. We began by recognizing a choice between a material process, a mental process and a relational process. We then subdivided material processes into action processes and event processes, and we subdivided mental processes into internalized processes and externalized processes. Action processes were further subdivided into intention processes and supervention processes. Internalized processes were further subdivided into perception processes, reaction processes and cognition processes.

In Section 8.4.4 we considered systems relating to the roles selected by a speaker for himself and his hearer. We began by recognizing a choice between indicative and imperative. Indicative was subdivided into declarative and interrogative. Imperative was subdivided into exclusive imperative and inclusive imperative. Interrogative was further subdivided into closed interrogative and open interrogative.

What we were doing in each of Sections 8.4.1 and 8.4.4 (and indeed in other subsections of 8.4) was to take a general area of meaning and gradually break it down into smaller and smaller sub-areas. In each section we were gradually making finer and finer distinctions in meaning; that is, we were gradually making more *delicate* distinctions in meaning.

We can arrange systems on a scale according to the fineness of the distinctions in meaning which they represent. This scale is called the scale of *delicacy*.

For instance the systems introduced in Section 8.4.1 can be arranged as shown in Figure 9.1. Similarly the systems introduced in Section 8.4.4 can be arranged as shown in Figure 9.2. In each case the least delicate systems are on the left of the diagram, the most delicate systems are on the right.

FIGURE 9.1   *The Relative Delicacy of the Transitivity Systems Which Relate to Types of Process*

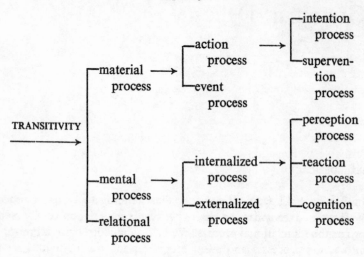

FIGURE 9.2   *The Relative Delicacy of the Mood Systems*

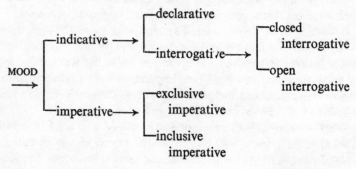

Each of the systems shown in Figures 9.1 and 9.2 consists of terms which are distinct, distinguishable and unified meanings and yet which are divisible into other distinct, distinguishable and unified meanings.

For instance material process, mental process and relational process are distinct and distinguishable meanings. Each is a unified meaning in the sense that, for example, all material processes have something in common; all material processes are alike in their 'materialness'. Similarly all mental processes have something in common; they are all alike in their 'mentalness'. And all relational processes have something in common; they are all alike in their 'relationalness'.

Yet, although each of these terms is a unified meaning, it is still possible to subdivide the term. Although, for instance, all material processes have their 'materialness' in common, although they are alike in being distinguishable from mental processes and relational processes, they still differ among themselves. As we have seen, material processes can be subdivided into action processes and event processes.

The generalizations made about systems in the first three sections of Chapter 8 remain true for the systems which have been discussed since then. It is still true that the terms in a system are distinct and distinguishable meanings between which it is possible to choose, that the meanings contrast with each other within a common area of meaning, that the terms are both mutually exclusive and mutually dependent and that the system is finite. However, we now also have to take account of the fact that a term in a system may itself be the common area of meaning for the terms of another system.

9.2 DEPENDENCY

It is also still true that the terms in a system not only contrast with each other within a common area of meaning but also contrast with each other within a common grammatical framework.

The term indicative and the term imperative are both applicable to the clause. Both are applicable only to clauses which are acting as the α elements of sentences. These two terms share a common grammatical framework which can be specified by reference to the entry conditions of the system.

The terms declarative and interrogative also share a common grammatical framework which can be specified by reference to their system's entry conditions. So too do the terms exclusive imperative and inclusive imperative. So too do the terms closed interrogative and open interrogative. We can, in fact, say of each of the systems shown in Figure 9.2 that the system's terms share a grammatical framework which can be specified by reference to the system's entry conditions.

As far as unit and structural environment are concerned, it so happens that all the systems shown in Figure 9.2 have the same entry conditions. All the systems are applicable to the clause. All are applicable only to clauses which are acting as α elements of sentences.

However as far as entry conditions provided by other systems are concerned, the systems shown in Figure 9.2 differ from each other.

The system declarative/interrogative, although like the system indicative/imperative in having an α clause as entry condition, differs from the system indicative/imperative in having an extra systemic entry condition. Before a choice can be made between declarative and interrogative, the term indicative must have been chosen from the indicative/imperative system.

The system exclusive imperative/inclusive imperative also differs from the system indicative/imperative in having an extra systemic entry condition. In this case, before a choice can be made between exclusive imperative and inclusive imperative, the term imperative must have been chosen from the indicative/imperative system.

The system closed interrogative/open interrogative differs from the system indicative/imperative in having two extra systemic entry conditions. Before a choice can be made between closed interrogative and open interrogative, the term indicative must have been chosen from the indicative/imperative system and the term interrogative must have been chosen from the declarative/interrogative system.

What is really happening here is that in each case a term from a system to the left of Figure 9.2 is providing an entry condition for a system further to the right. Systems to the right of the diagram are *dependent* on those further to the left in that choices between their terms can only be made if particular terms have been chosen from the systems to the left.

Delicacy is not just a matter of the fineness of semantic distinctions; it is also a matter of dependency. The systems to the right of Figure 9.2 are more delicate than those to the left, not only in that they represent finer semantic distinctions, but also in that they are dependent on those to the left.

Similarly the systems to the right of Figure 9.1 are more delicate than those to the left not only in that they represent finer semantic distinctions, but also in that they are dependent on those to the left.

Dependency relationships such as that between the system closed interrogative/open interrogative and the term interrogative and that between the system exclusive imperative/inclusive imperative and the term imperative are perhaps self-evident from the semantic relationship which exists between them.

However not all dependency relationships are accompanied by semantic relationships of the kind that exist between the systems of Figure 9.2 (and between the systems of Figure 9.1). Sometimes a system is dependent on a term with which it has little or nothing in common in the way of meaning.

For instance, as was shown in Chapter 8, the term finite from the system of finiteness is an entry condition to the mood systems. The mood systems are dependent on the term finite even though they have relatively little in common with the term finite in the way of meaning. As shown in Figure 9.3 the mood systems are more delicate than the system of finiteness, in that they are dependent on the system of finiteness, even though they have no close semantic relationship with the system of finiteness.

FIGURE 9.3   *The Relative Delicacy of the Systems*
of Finiteness and Mood

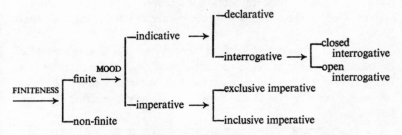

(It is perhaps necessary at this point to make explicit the notational conventions which have been used so far in this chapter:

$$\longrightarrow \left[\begin{array}{c} a \\ b \end{array} \right.$$

indicates that there is a system of terms such that either term a or term b must be chosen.

$$\longrightarrow \left[\begin{array}{c} a \\ b \end{array} \right. \longrightarrow \left[\begin{array}{c} c \\ d \end{array} \right.$$

indicates that term a acts as an entry condition for a further system with the terms c and d. The system c/d is dependent on the system a/b and, this being so, the system c/d is more delicate than the system a/b.)

9.3 SIMULTANEITY

It was stressed in Section 9.2 that the terms in a system contrast with each other within a common grammatical framework. It was implied that this common grammatical framework can be divided into two levels: a level which can be specified by way of reference to unit and structural environment; and a level which can be specified by way of reference to systemic environment (by reference, that is, to the relationships which exist between the system under consideration and other systems). Section 9.3, like Section 9.2, will be largely concerned with the latter of the two levels.

The relationship between systems and the former of the two levels of their grammatical framework will be further discussed in Volume II Chapter 2.

In Section 9.2 it was shown that one possible kind of relationship between a system and the other systems in its systemic environment was that of dependency. In Section 9.3 it will be shown that there is another kind of relationship possible between systems, that of *simultaneity*.

A system is *simultaneous* with another system if it is independent of the other system but has the same entry conditions as the other system. When two systems are simultaneous their terms can combine freely; any term from one system can combine with any term from the other system.

For example, the system unrestricted process/restricted process (discussed in Section 8.4.2) is simultaneous with the system action process/ event process (discussed in Section 8.4.1). The two systems are independent of each other; it is not necessary for a particular term to have been chosen from one of the systems in order for a choice to be possible between the terms of the other system.

The two systems have the same entry conditions: both are applicable to the clause; and for both it is necessary for the term material process to have been chosen in preference to mental process or relational process.

The terms of the two systems combine freely: a material process clause can choose unrestricted process or restricted process regardless of whether it chooses action process or event process; it can choose action process or event process regardless of whether it chooses unrestricted process or restricted process. Of the clauses

Ex. 9.1   *The lieutenant marched his prisoners away*

Ex. 9.2   *The prisoners marched away*

Ex. 9.3   *A violent downpour has flooded the river*

Ex. 9.4   *This stream floods (every time it rains)*

Ex. 9.5   *John kicked the door*
Ex. 9.6   *Lambs skip friskily*
Ex. 9.7   *The landslide engulfed the cottage*
Ex. 9.8   *This stream flows peacefully*

Exs 9.1 and 9.2 have combined the term unrestricted process with the term action process, Exs 9.3 and 9.4 have combined the term unrestricted process with the term event process, Exs 9.5 and 9.6 have combined the term restricted process with the term action process and Exs 9.7 and 9.8 have combined the term restricted process with the term event process.

The simultaneity of the system unrestricted process/restricted process and the system action process/event process is shown in Figure 9.4.

FIGURE 9.4   *The Simultaneity of the System*
Unrestricted Process/Restricted Process and the System Action
Process/Event Process

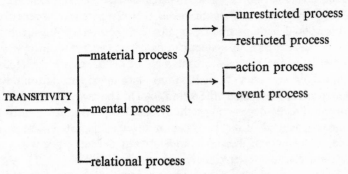

(A bracket of the type shown in Figure 9.4 is used to show the simultaneity of systems.)

When specifying the systemic environment of a system it is necessary not only to show the systems on which the given system depends, but also to show the systems with whose terms the terms of the given system can combine; that is, to show the systems with which the given system is simultaneous.

The use of the word *simultaneous* is not intended to imply that there is anything chronological about the scale of delicacy. It would be most misleading to suggest that simultaneous choices are made at the same point in time but that dependent choices are made after each other in time. All the choices made by a given clause are of course simultaneous in the chronological sense. When used in relation to systems the word *simultaneous* implies having the same degree of dependency. Simultaneous systems are dependent on the same other systems. They occur at the same point on the scale of delicacy.

9.4 COMPLEX DEPENDENCY

In this chapter, then, we are concerned with relationships between systems. Just as the scale of rank relates units to each other, so the scale of delicacy relates systems to each other. We have seen that there are semantic relationships between systems, and environmental relationships between systems. We have seen that, although environmental relationships usually reflect semantic relationships, they do not always do so. We have seen that the environmental relationships are basically of two kinds: dependency and simultaneity.

The notion of dependency needs to be further explored. We must distinguish between different degrees and different kinds of dependency.

We should perhaps first distinguish between direct dependency and indirect dependency. A system is directly dependent on the system immediately to the left of it on the scale of delicacy. It is indirectly dependent on any system more than one place to the left of it on the scale of delicacy. For instance the system closed interrogative/open interrogative is directly dependent on the system declarative/interrogative. It is indirectly dependent on the system indicative/imperative. The dependence on the system indicative/imperative is indirect since it is via the system declarative/interrogative.

.A system on which a given system is directly dependent provides the *point of entry* to the given system, the point of entry to a system being the most immediate of the system's entry conditions.

The entry conditions to the system closed interrogative/open interrogative include: the clause; that the clause must be acting as an α element; that indicative must have been chosen in preference to imperative; that interrogative must have been chosen in preference to declarative. Of these entry conditions the most immediate, the point of entry to the system, is the term interrogative. It is immediately to the left of the system closed interrogative/open interrogative on the scale of delicacy. It is the entry condition which most successfully differentiates the delicacy of the system closed interrogative/open interrogative from the delicacy of other systems; the system closed interrogative/open interrogative shares with the system declarative/interrogative all its entry conditions except the term interrogative.

The point of entry is the most useful entry condition to state in relation to any system. Since a system shares with its point of entry all its entry conditions except the point of entry itself, reference to the point of entry not only specifies the distinguishing entry condition but also implies all the other entry conditions.

Secondly we should distinguish between simple direct dependency and complex direct dependency. In simple dependency a given system is directly dependent on only one other system. This one other system provides the only possible point of entry to the given system. For example, there is simple dependency between the system closed interrogative/open interrogative and the system declarative/interrogative. The system closed interrogative/open interrogative is directly dependent on the system declarative interrogative and on no other. The choice of interrogative from the system declarative/interrogative is the only way of entering the system closed interrogative/open interrogative; the only way, that is, of making possible a choice between the terms of the system closed interrogative/open interrogative.

There are two kinds of complex direct dependency: an 'either . . . or' kind and a 'both . . . and' kind.

In the 'either . . . or' kind of complex direct dependency, there are alternative systems on which a given system may depend. There are alternative points of entry to the given system. For instance the system active/passive (discussed in Section 8.4.2) is dependent on the system transitive/intransitive. The choice of the term transitive in preference to intransitive provides a point of entry to the system active/passive. However this is not the only way in to the system active/passive. The choice of causative in preference to non-causative also provides a point of entry to the system active/passive, and so too does the choice of untypical middle in preference to typical middle. There are three possible points of entry to the system active/passive and if any one of the three is chosen then a choice between the terms of the system active/ passive becomes possible.

The clauses

Ex. 9.9   *John threw the ball*
Ex. 9.10   *The ball was thrown by John*

have chosen transitive. The choice of transitive made possible a choice between the terms of the system active/passive. Ex. 9.9 has chosen active. Ex. 9.10 has chosen passive.

The clauses

Ex. 8.35   *John opened the door*
Ex. 9.11   *The door was opened by John*

have chosen causative. The choice of causative made possible a choice between the terms of the system active/passive. Ex. 8.35 has chosen active. Ex. 9.11 has chosen passive.

The clauses

Ex. 8.60   *Her excited daughter danced Mary round the room*
Ex. 9.12   *Mary was danced round the room by her excited daughter*

have chosen untypical middle. The choice of untypical middle made possible a choice between the terms of the system active/passive. Ex. 8.60 has chosen active. Ex. 9.12 has chosen passive.

The relationship between the system active/passive and the systems on which it depends is shown in Figure 9.5.

FIGURE 9.5   *The Active/Passive System and the Systems
on Which It Depends*

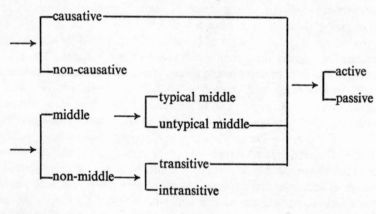

(The notation

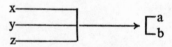

is used to indicate that a system has more than one possible point of entry. Here, the three parallel lines leading to the arrow indicate that the system a/b has three possible points of entry: x or y or z.)

In the 'both ... and' kind of complex dependency we again find that a given system is dependent on more than one other system. Again there is more than one point of entry to the given system. However, whereas in the 'either . . . or' kind of complex dependency the points of entry are alternatives, in the 'both . . . and' kind of complex dependency the points of entry are complementary; that is, whereas in the 'either . . . or' kind of complex dependency only one of the possible entry points need be chosen in order to make possible a choice between the terms of the given system, in the 'both . . . and' kind of complex dependency all the entry points must be chosen before a choice becomes possible between the terms of the given system.

For instance we may now qualify the statement made in Section 8.4.1 to the effect that clauses which had chosen event process could not make a choice between intention process and supervention process. Certainly it is usually true that such clauses cannot choose between intention process and supervention process. However, if a clause has not only chosen event process but has also chosen untypical animacy (that is, if it has an animate participant in the role of actor instead of the more usual inanimate participant), a choice between intention process and supervention process then becomes possible. Event process and untypical animacy are complementary entry points to the system intention process/supervention process. For a choice to be possible between intention process and supervention process, both event process and untypical animacy must have been chosen. Event process is no use without untypical animacy when it comes to providing an entry point for the system intention process/supervention process.

The clauses

Ex. 8.15   *A stream flows through that part of the valley*
Ex. 8.20   *The car backfired noisily*

have chosen event process. However, since they have not also chosen untypical animacy, they are unable to choose from the system intention process/supervention process.

The clauses

Ex. 9.13   *Stealthily Theodore flowed into the room*
Ex. 9.14   *but (on seeing the bishop) ebbed again hastily*

have chosen both event process and untypical animacy. They are therefore able to choose from the system intention process/supervention process. They have in fact chosen intention process.

The relationship between the system intention process/supervention process and the systems on which it depends is shown in Figure 9.6.

FIGURE 9.6   *The Intention Process/Supervention*
          Process System and the Systems on Which It Depends

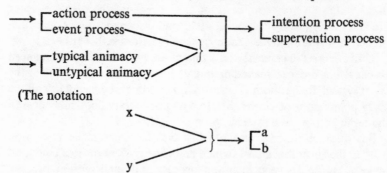

(The notation

is used to indicate that a system has complementary points of entry.
Here the system a/b has two complementary points of entry. Both x and
y must be chosen in order that a choice between a and b may be possible.)

Readers are reminded that, as stated in Chapter 8, once a choice
between the terms of a system is possible it is also obligatory; one or
other of the terms must be chosen.

As can be seen from Figure 9.6, the system intention process/
supervention process, as well as providing an example of the 'both
. . . and' kind of complex dependency, provides a further example
of the 'either . . . or' kind of complex dependency. There are two
alternative entry points to the system: the choice of action process;
and the choice of event process combined with the choice of untypical animacy. The latter is of course the example of the 'both . . .
and' kind of complex dependency which has just been discussed.

9.5 NETWORKS

Systems can be grouped into *networks*.

A network is a set of systems which are closely related from a semantic point of view. For instance the transitivity and voice systems form a
network since they are all concerned with processes, participants and
circumstances. The theme systems form a network since they are all
concerned with the giving of prominence. The mood and modality systems form a network since they are all concerned with attitudes adopted
by the speaker or writer. The episode linkage systems form a network
since they are all concerned with relationships between episodes.

These networks are exemplified in Figures 9.7 to 9.10.

FIGURE 9.7

The Transitivity and Voice Network

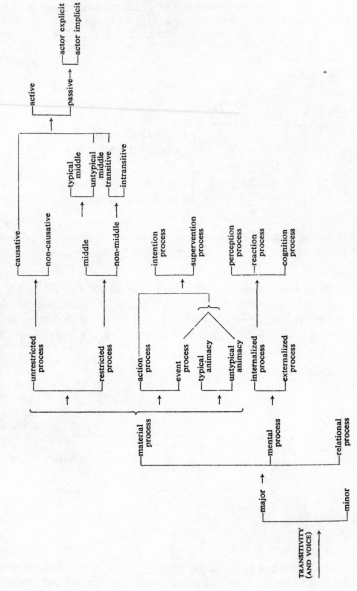

It must be stressed that the versions of the networks given in Figures 9.7 to 9.10 are far from complete. The diagrams include only those systems which were introduced in Section 8.4. As was pointed out in Section 8.4, these systems represent only a small proportion of the systems which could have been discussed under their respective headings.

FIGURE 9.8   *The Theme Network*

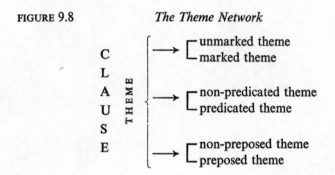

As well as being closely related from a semantic point of view, the systems of a network also show a high degree of interrelatedness from an environmental point of view. Certainly it is true that there are instances of a system depending on a system from a network other than

FIGURE 9.9   *The Mood and Modality Network*

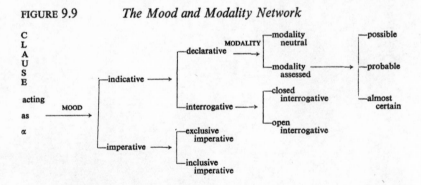

its own, as for example the dependency of the mood systems on the system of finiteness. But compared with the intricate pattern of dependencies which exists within a network, the examples of dependencies between networks are few and far between.

The systems of a network usually share those of their entry conditions which are specified by reference to unit and structural environment.

FIGURE 9.10

The Episode Linkage Network

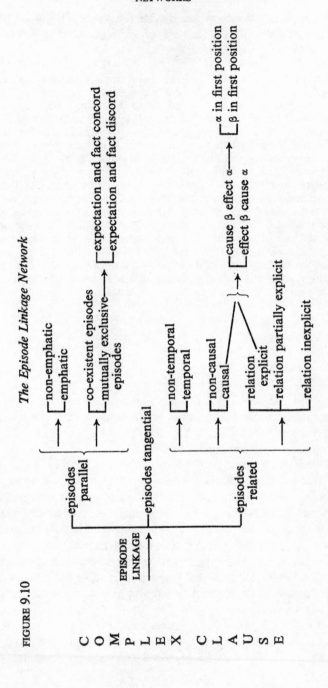

Such entry conditions are usually referred to collectively as the *point of origin* of the network. (The point of origin is usually shown down the left-hand side of a network diagram.)

It is perhaps worthwhile at this point to summarize what has been said about different kinds of entry condition to systems. In Chapter 8 the entry conditions were divided into three kinds: those specified by reference to unit; those specified by reference to structural environment; those specified by reference to systemic environment. In Chapter 9 the first two of these kinds have been grouped together and opposed to the third. (As was implied in Chapter 8 the difference between the first two is really a difference in generality rather than a difference in kind.) We now see that the first two kinds, still grouped together, now under the heading of *point of origin*, apply to whole networks of systems, while the third kind has to be discussed in relation to individual systems within a network. (The difference between on the one hand the first two kinds and on the other hand the third kind is a difference in generality as well as a difference in kind.) We saw in Section 9.4 that the most important of the systemic entry conditions to an individual system within a network is the one that has been called the *point of entry* to the system.

9.6 DISCUSSION

9.6.1 *General Linguistics*

We saw in Chapters 5, 6 and 7 that language was patterned at the level of grammar and that it was through its regularity and patterning that language was able to work. We saw that all languages were alike in having patterning and regularity.

In Chapters 5, 6 and 7 we were mainly concerned with the more surface kinds of grammatical patterning. In Chapters 8 and 9 we have been concerned with a more fundamental kind of grammatical patterning. We have seen that the meanings which can be expressed by the grammar of a language do not just exist each in isolation. Language is structured semantically as well as formally. It is through its semantic regularity and patterning as well as through its formal regularity and patterning that language is able to work. All languages are alike not only in having formal regularity and patterning but also in having semantic regularity and patterning.

In Chapters 5, 6 and 7 the formal structures of grammar, the more surface patterns of grammar, were discussed mainly in terms of patterns along the axis of chain. In Chapters 8 and 9 the semantic structure of grammar has been discussed mainly in terms of contrasting choices. We have been exploring further the point made in Chapter 4, that language works by means of contrasting choices.

9.6.2 *Descriptive Linguistics*

When we are describing a language (or a variety of a language) one of the things we have to do, perhaps the most important thing we have to do, is to codify the *meaning potential* of the grammar of that language. That is, we have to show what meanings it is possible for the grammar of the language to express and how these meanings relate to each other. We also want to show how the meanings relate to the more surface aspects of the grammar; we therefore select a method of codification which will enable us to do this.

It is this method of codification that we have been considering in Chapters 8 and 9. We codify the meaning potential of the grammar of a language by means of systems and system networks. The networks given in Figures 9.7, 9.8, 9.9 and 9.10 are, in fact, codifications of parts of the meaning potential of the English language.

When we are describing a whole language (or a whole variety of a language) we are mainly concerned with meaning potential. When we are describing a particular stretch of language we are usually more concerned with actual meaning.

When describing a particular stretch of language we have to state what meanings have actually been chosen by that stretch of language. A statement of the meanings which have been chosen from a network by a particular stretch of language is called a *selection expression*.

The selection expression which shows what choices from the transitivity and voice network have been made by

Ex. 8.10   *Theodore saw Mary on Tuesday*

is {major : mental process : internalized process : perception process}.

The selection expression which shows what choices from the theme network have been made by

Ex. 8.76   *It was Peter who swam the fastest*

is {{unmarked theme / predicated theme / non-preposed theme}}.

The selection expression which shows what choices from the mood and modality network have been made by

Ex. 8.112   *That may be John*

is {indicative : declarative : modality assessed : possible}.

The selection expression which shows what choices from the episode linkage network have been made by

Ex. 8.120 *Since the availability of the pitch is uncertain, the committee have postponed the match against the next village*

is {episodes related : {non-temporal / causal : I; cause β effect α : β in first position / relation explicit : I;}}

(The notational conventions used in selection expressions are as follows:

: indicates that the term that follows the symbol is from a system which is dependent on the term which precedes the symbol;

/ indicates simultaneity between terms;

: I; . . . : I; indicates complex dependency of the 'both . . . and' kind. The term which precedes the first occurrence of this symbol combines with the term which precedes the second occurrence of the symbol to provide the point of entry to the system from which comes the term which follows the first occurrence of the symbol;

{. . .} is used in two ways. It is used to enclose a whole selection expression. It is also used to enclose a simultaneous set of terms within a selection expression.)

As has been said, when we are describing a particular stretch of language we are usually more concerned with actual meaning than with potential meaning. However it is important to realize that actual meaning can only be fully appreciated in relation to potential meaning. As pointed out in Chapter 8, in order to fully understand the meaning of something, we need to know what it does not mean as well as what it does mean. Systems and system networks are therefore just as relevant to the description of particular stretches of language as to the description of whole languages and varieties of languages.

We are here considering the 'does' in the light of the 'can do', or more specifically the 'means' in the light of the 'can mean'. (See 2.1.)

9.6.3 *Contrastive Linguistics*

When comparing and contrasting two different languages we should expect them to be similar in their semantic structure, most of the differences between them lying in the more surface aspects of their grammar.

Even more confidently we should expect the differences between two regional dialects of a language to lie in the surface aspects of their grammar rather than in the more fundamental aspects.

When studying the history of a language we should expect to find that what has remained constant between two historical phases of the language is the semantic structure, while what have changed are some features of the surface aspects of the grammar. (Professor Halliday has cast doubt on this last hypothesis with reference to the history of English.)[1]

When comparing and contrasting two different registers or two different idiolects we should again expect to find that they are similar in semantic structure but differ in some of the surface aspects of their grammar.

We should also expect to find another kind of difference. We should expect to find a difference in the frequency with which the registers (or idiolects) select a particular option from among the potential meanings of the language. We should expect, for instance, that advertising language would select imperative in preference to indicative more frequently than would most written registers. We should expect that scientific language would select passive in preference to active more frequently than would most registers. Furthermore we should expect that a higher proportion of passive clauses in scientific language would choose actor implicit in preference to actor explicit than would be the case in other registers.

It is possible that social dialects may also differ in the frequency with which they select particular options.

9.6.4   *Applied Linguistics*

An example of the use of systems and system networks in a sociolinguistic study can be found in the work of Mr G. J. Turner who has been investigating the grammatical options selected by children from different social backgrounds.[2]

This research is also relevant to the teaching of English as a native language.

An example of the use of systems and system networks in a literary study can be found in Professor Halliday's work on William Golding's *The Inheritors*.[3]

---

[1] Halliday (forthcoming)   [2] Turner (1972)   [3] Halliday (1971)

9.6.5   *Systemic Linguistics and Other Schools of Linguistics*

Systemic linguistics is like other schools of linguistics in recognizing that language is semantically[1] structured as well as formally structured.

It differs from other schools in the way in which it codifies the semantic structure. It differs from other schools in that it views the semantic structure of a language as a set of related choices. It also differs from other schools in the way in which it relates the semantic structure of a language to the formal structure, as will be explained in Volume II.

---

[1] Not all systemic linguists would be happy with the term *semantically* in this connection. See Volume II Chapter 6.

Bibliography

CHAPTERS 1 AND 2

BERNSTEIN B. (ed.) (1971) *Class, Codes and Control, Vol. 1* and (1972) *Vol. 2*, London: Routledge & Kegan Paul

CHOMSKY, N. (1957) *Syntactic Structures*, The Hague: Mouton

CRYSTAL, D. (1968) *What Is Linguistics?*, London: Arnold

—— (1971) *Linguistics*, Harmondsworth: Penguin Books

DOUGHTY, P. S., PEARCE, J. and THORNTON, G. (1971) *Language in Use*, London: Arnold

FILLMORE, C. J. (1968) 'The Case for Case' in Bach, E. and Harms, R. T. (eds) *Universals in Linguistic Theory*, New York: Holt, Rinehart & Winston

FIRTH, J. R. (1957) *Papers in Linguistics, 1934–1951*, London: OUP

HALLIDAY, M. A. K. (1961) 'Categories of the Theory of Grammar', *Word*, XVII, 241–92

—— (1969) 'Relevant Models of Language' in *The State of Language* (*Educational Review*, XXII, 26–37, University of Birmingham School of Education)

—— (1971a) 'Language in a Social Perspective' in *The Context of Language* (*Educational Review*, XXIII, 165–88. University of Birmingham School of Education)

—— (1971b) 'Linguistic Function and Literary Style: An inquiry into the language of William Golding's *The Inheritors*' in Chatman, S. (ed.) *The Proceedings of the Second Style in Language Conference* (*Bellagio, 1969*), London: OUP

—— (forthcoming) *An Outlook on Modern English*, London: OUP

——, MCINTOSH, A. and STREVENS, P. D. (1964) *The Linguistic Sciences and Language Teaching*, London: Longmans

HUDDLESTON, R. D., HUDSON, R. A., WINTER, E. O. and HENRICI, A. (1968) *Sentence and Clause in Scientific English*, University College, London: mimeographed

HUDSON, R. A. (1971) *English Complex Sentences*, Amsterdam: North-Holland

LAMB, S. M. (1966) *Outline of Stratificational Grammar*, Washington, DC: Georgetown University Press

LEECH, G. N. (1966) *English in Advertising*, London: Longmans
—— (1969) *A Linguistic Guide to English Poetry*, London: Longmans
LYONS, J. (1970a) *Chomsky*, London: Collins
—— (ed.) (1970b) *New Horizons in Linguistics*, Harmondsworth: Penguin Books
MUIR, J. (1972) *A Modern Approach to English Grammar*, London: Batsford
PIKE, K. L. (1967) *Language in Relation to a Unified Theory of Human Behaviour* (Janua Linguarum, Series Major, 24), 2nd rev. edn, The Hague: Mouton
SAUSSURE, F. DE (1916) *Cours de linguistique générale*, Paris: Payot
SINCLAIR, J. MCH. (1965) *A Course in Spoken English, 3: Grammar*, prepub. edn and (1972) rev. edn, London: OUP

In writing these introductory chapters, the author has been indebted directly or indirectly to all the above-listed works, particularly to Halliday, 1971a.

Suggestions for further reading have been given in the text of Chapters 1 and 2.

Works which have become available since the writing of this book was completed include the following:

FAWCETT, R. (1973a) *Systemic Functional Grammar in A Cognitive Model of Language*, University College, London: mimeographed
—— (1973b) *Generating a Sentence in Systemic Functional Grammar*, University College, London: mimeographed
HALLIDAY, M. A. K. (1963) *Explorations in the Functions of Language*, London: Arnold
WINOGRAD, T. (1972) *Understanding Natural Language*, Edinburgh: The University Press

All these works include interesting theoretical discussions of systemic linguistics. In addition Halliday, 1973 is particularly relevant to the systemic interest in the sociological aspects of language. (Halliday, 1973 includes a reprint of Halliday, 1969, Halliday, 1971a and Halliday, 1971b together with other papers.) Fawcett, 1973a and b and Winograd, 1972 are relevant to the recent interest among systemic linguists in the psychological aspects of language. Winograd, 1972 is relevant to the application of linguistic theory to work on computers and the application of computers to work on linguistic theory.

CHAPTER 3

ELLIS, J. (1966) 'On Contextual Meaning' in Bazell, C. E., Catford, J. C., Halliday, M. A. K. and Robins, R. H. (eds) *In Memory of J. R. Firth*, London: Longmans
FIRTH, J. R. (1957) 'Modes of Meaning' in Firth, J. R. *Papers in Linguistics, 1934–1951*, London: OUP
HALLIDAY, M. A. K. (1961) 'Categories of the Theory of Grammar', *Word*, XVII, 241–92
——, MCINTOSH, A. and STREVENS, P. D. (1964) *The Linguistic Sciences and Language Teaching*, London: Longmans

The main sources for this chapter are Halliday, 1961 and Halliday *et al.*, 1964. The discussion of the subdivisions of situation is based on a talk given by Dr Jeffrey Ellis to the Linguistics Association of Great Britain, May 1962. The ideas put forward in this talk were later elaborated and written up in Ellis, 1966.

Historically, the systemic linguists' concept of level of language can be traced back through scale-and-category linguistics to the work of Professor J. R. Firth, as shown, for example, in Firth, 1957.

CHAPTER 4

HALLIDAY, M. A. K., MCINTOSH, A. and STREVENS, P. D. (1964) *The Linguistic Sciences and Language Teaching,* London: Longmans
LEECH, G. N. (1969) *A Linguistic Guide to English Poetry*, London: Longmans

The main sources for this chapter are Halliday *et al.*, 1964 and a talk given by Professor M. A. K. Halliday to the Linguistics Association of Great Britain November 1963. The discussion of latent patterns is based on a talk given by Professor J. McH. Sinclair to the Hull Linguistic Circle, February 1963. Similar ideas are discussed in Leech, 1969.

CHAPTER 5

HALLIDAY, M. A. K. (1961) 'Categories of the Theory of Grammar', *Word*, XVII, 241–92
—— (1970) 'Language Structure and Language Function' in Lyons, J. (ed.) *New Horizons in Linguistics*, Harmondsworth: Penguin Books
——, MCINTOSH, A. and STREVENS, P. D. (1964) *The Linguistic Sciences and Language Teaching*, London: Longmans
HUDDLESTON, R. D. (1965) 'Rank and Depth', *Language*, XLI, 574–86
MUIR, J. (1972) *A Modern Approach to English Grammar*, London: Batsford
SINCLAIR, J. MCH. (1965) *A Course in Spoken English. 3: Grammar*, prepub. edn and (1972) rev. edn, London: OUP

The main sources for this chapter are Halliday, 1961, Halliday *et al.*, 1964, Halliday, 1970 and Sinclair, 1965. (Sinclair, 1972 was published just as the present book was on the point of going to press.)

The discussion of depth (Section 5.3) is based on Huddleston, 1965.

More comprehensive treatments of the structure of English grammar than have been given here can be found in Sinclair, 1972 and Muir, 1972. (Readers may find it interesting to compare Sinclair 1972 and Muir 1972 in order to see how far two descriptions of the same language based on the same model of language agree with each other and how far they differ.)

CHAPTER 6

HALLIDAY, M. A. K. (1961) 'Categories of the Theory of Grammar', *Word*, XVII, 241–92
—— (1965) 'Types of Structure' (*Nuffield Programme in Linguistics and English Teaching Work Paper I*), University College, London: mimeographed
——, MCINTOSH, A. and STREVENS, P. D. (1964) *The Linguistic Sciences and Language Teaching*, London: Longmans
HUDDLESTON, R. D. (1965) 'Rank and Depth', *Language*, XLI, 574–86

The main sources for the first section of this chapter are Halliday, 1961 and Halliday *et al.*, 1964. The main sources for the second section are Huddleston, 1965 and Halliday, 1965

CHAPTER 7

CATFORD, J. C. (1965) *A Linguistic Theory of Translation* London: OUP
HALLIDAY, M. A. K. (1961) 'Categories of the Theory of Grammar', *Word*, XVII, 241–92
—— (1965) 'Types of Structure' (*Nuffield Programme in Linguistics and English Teaching Work Paper I*), University College, London: mimeographed
—— (1966) 'The Concept of Rank: A reply', *Journal of Linguistics*, II, 110–18
——, MCINTOSH, A. and STREVENS, P. D. (1964) *The Linguistic Sciences and Language Teaching*, London: Longmans
HUDDLESTON, R. D. (1965) 'Rank and Depth', *Language*, XLI, 574–86
MATTHEWS, P. H. (1966) 'The Concept of Rank in "Neo-Firthian" Grammar', *Journal of Linguistics*, II, 101–10

The main sources for this chapter are Halliday, 1961; Halliday *et al.*, 1964; Huddleston, 1965; Halliday, 1965; and Halliday, 1966.
Some of the objections which have been raised to certain aspects of unit and rank can be found in Matthews, 1966. A reply to these objections, a reply which the writer of the present book finds convincing, is given in Halliday, 1966.
The discussion of translation referred to in Section 7.4.4 can be found in Catford, 1965.

CHAPTER 8

HALLIDAY, M. A. K. (1961) 'Categories of the Theory of Grammar', *Word*, XVII, 241–92
—— (1966) 'Some Notes on "Deep" Grammar', *Journal of Linguistics*, II, 57–67
—— (1967a) *Some Aspects of the Thematic Organisation of the English Clause*, Santa Monica, California: The Rand Corporation

—— (1967b) 'Notes on Transitivity and Theme in English', Part I, *Journal of Linguistics*, III, 37–81; (1967c) Part II, *Journal of Linguistics*, III, 199–244 and (1968) Part III, *Journal of Linguistics*, IV, 179–215

—— (1970a) 'Language Structure and Language Function' in Lyons, J. (ed.) *New Horizons in Linguistics*, Harmondsworth: Penguin Books

—— (1970b) 'Functional Diversity in Language As Seen from a Consideration of Modality and Mood in English', *Foundations of Language*, VI, 322–61

—— (forthcoming) *An Outlook on Modern English*, London: OUP

——, MCINTOSH, A. and STREVENS, P. D. (1964) *The Linguistic Sciences and Language Teaching*, London: Longmans

HUDSON, R. A. (1969) *Types of Co-ordination Relation in English*, University College, London: mimeographed

MUIR, J. (1972) *A Modern Approach to English Grammar*, London: Batsford

SINCLAIR, J. MCH. (1965) *A Course in Spoken English. 3: Grammar*, prepub. edn and (1972) rev. edn, London: OUP

The main sources for this chapter are Halliday, 1961; Halliday *et al.*, 1964; Halliday, 1966; and Halliday, 1970a. The main sources for Sections 8.4.1 and 8.4.2 are Halliday, 1967b; Halliday, 1968; and Halliday, forthcoming. Main sources for Section 8.4.3 are Halliday, 1967c; Halliday, 1968; and Halliday 1967a. Main source for Section 8.4.5 is Halliday, 1970b. Relevant to Section 8.4.6 is Hudson, 1969. Discussion of some systems mentioned only briefly in this chapter and of some systems not mentioned at all can be found in Muir, 1972 and Sinclair, 1965 and 1972.

The introductory nature of the accounts of systems given in this chapter must again be stressed. Readers of the chapter are strongly advised to read also the books listed in the above bibliography, particularly Halliday, 1970a; Halliday, 1967b; Halliday, 1967c; Halliday, 1968; and Halliday, 1970b (also Halliday, forthcoming, when it becomes available).

CHAPTER 9

HALLIDAY, M. A. K. (1966) 'Some Notes on "Deep" Grammar', *Journal of Linguistics*, II, 57–67

—— (1967a) 'Notes on Transitivity and Theme in English', Part I, *Journal of Linguistics*, III, 37–81; (1967b) Part II, *Journal of Linguistics*, III, 199–244 and (1968) Part III, *Journal of Linguistics*, IV, 179–215

—— (1970) 'Functional Diversity in Language As Seen from a Consideration of Modality and Mood in English', *Foundations of Language*, VI, 322–61

—— (1971) 'Linguistic Function and Literary Style: An inquiry into the language of William Golding's *The Inheritors*' in Chatman, S. (ed.) *The Proceedings of the Second Style in Language Conference* (*Bellagio, 1969*), London: OUP

—— (forthcoming) *An Outlook on Modern English*, London: OUP

HUDDLESTON, R. D., HUDSON, R. A., WINTER, E. O. and HENRICI, A. (1968) *Sentence and Clause in Scientific English*, University College, London: mimeographed

HUDDLESTON, R. D. and UREN, ORMOND (1969) 'Declarative, Interrogative and Imperative in French', *Lingua* XXII

TURNER, G. J. (1972) 'Social Class and Children's Language of Control at Age Five and Age Seven' in Bernstein, B. (ed.) *Class, Codes and Control, Vol. II: Applied studies towards a sociology of language*, London: Routledge & Kegan Paul

The main sources for this chapter are Halliday, 1966; Halliday, 1967a, 1967b and 1968; Halliday, 1970; and Halliday, forthcoming.

An example of a systemic description of a particular register can be found in Huddleston *et al.*, 1968. An example of the application of systemic analysis to a language other than English can be found in Huddleston and Uren, 1969. An example of a systemic sociolinguistic study can be found in Turner, 1972. An example of a systemic literary study can be found in Halliday, 1971.

Index

Index